HF
5549
.V29
1985

Van Dersal, William
Richard, 1907-

The successful
supervisor in
government and
business

DATE			

Business/Science/Technology
Division

© THE BAKER & TAYLOR CO.

THE SUCCESSFUL SUPERVISOR

The Successful Supervisor

IN GOVERNMENT AND BUSINESS

FOURTH EDITION

William R. Van Dersal

1817

HARPER & ROW, PUBLISHERS, New York
Cambridge, Philadelphia, San Francisco, London
Mexico City, São Paulo, Singapore, Sydney

To my wife, Eva

Library of Congress Cataloging-in-Publication Data

Van Dersal, William Richard, 1907–
   The successful supervisor in government and
business

   Bibliography: p.
   Includes index.
   1. Supervision of employees. I. Title.
HF5549.V29   1985   658.3′02   85–42595
ISBN 0–06–015476–4

85 86 87 88 89 HC 10 9 8 7 6 5 4 3 2 1

Contents

Preface

This book was written for practicing supervisors, whether in government, business, industry, or elsewhere, and whether in high positions or low. Supervision has to do with influencing human action in organizations doing work. The policies and procedures of these organizations may differ widely and so may their objectives, but scarcely the fundamental nature of their supervisory problems.

There are no panaceas in this book, and its writer makes no claim to being an expert. What I have written here summarizes what I have learned over many years by observing, analyzing, and studying both successful and unsuccessful supervisors.

One of the things that helped me a great deal in this endeavor was a project undertaken in 1945 by T. Roy Reid, at that time director of personnel for the United States Department of Agriculture. He wrote a personal letter to each of some five hundred supervisors who were named as the best in that large department by their various bureau chiefs. He asked the supervisors to write him a letter explaining what they thought was most important in supervising people, and describing something of the methods and techniques used in their work.

The replies, from all parts of the country, made a stack about three feet high. This I remember well because I had the opportunity of studying these letters for months. Some were brief. Some were many pages in length, but all were sincere and packed with ideas. Gradually, I came to distinguish those key ideas which, if they appeared in one letter, were likely to appear in most or all of the others. These ideas, some seven in number, and common to the five hundred supervisors, are expressed in Chapter 2 as general principles.

Over the past thirty-six years I have discussed these ideas, or principles, as well as many other aspects of supervision, with thousands of supervisors—in the federal government, in state governments, in foreign governments, in businesses, and in industry. I have subjected the principles to critical discussion in dozens of formal management training courses, as well as in my classes in supervision at the Graduate School of the United States Department of Agriculture and at Colorado State University, Columbia University, North Carolina State University, and a number of others. Besides this, they have been reproduced and used in a large number of agencies of the federal government and in agencies of many foreign governments. All told, they have undergone a certain amount of modification, although the concepts they express have stood up remarkably well. In a very real sense, these ideas have been validated by tens of thousands of years of supervisory experience. This extensive testing should, I believe, generate reasonable confidence in their substance.

In addition to this experience, I have also been combing the literature for ideas and techniques of possible value to practicing supervisors. Whatever I have found that seemed of possible use I have promptly put to the test either in management and supervisory courses or classes, or in my own organization, or in both. It became clear to me long ago that there was a serious gap between academic theory and the everyday practice of supervision.[1] I found great difficulty in

1. Others have expressed this idea. For example, see Lyndall F. Urwick, "Management and Human Relations," in *Leadership and Organization*, by R. Tannenbaum, I. R. Wechsler, and F. Massarik (New York: McGraw-Hill

trying to bridge that gap. I suggest it as one reason why supervisors generally do not seem to be avid readers of the professional books in their field.

It has often seemed to me that the science of human relations—if, indeed, it may be called a science—is one of the poorest and most confused of them all. In fact, if there is any one thing that seems clear about us, it is that we do not yet seem to know how to get along with each other very well—at work, at home, in private life, in public life, in our own country, or as between nations. Since most adult Americans work, and since nearly all of them are supervised in their work, or supervise others, perhaps attempting to improve the quality of supervision could have an important effect on human relations in general. However, I have had no such project in mind. If I can help supervisors at least to approach their supervisory tasks and problems on a common-sense, intelligent basis, I shall have succeeded in achieving the goal I had in mind when I collected the material for and wrote this book.

The fact is that supervisors bear a heavy responsibility that too few of them seem to realize. The way a supervisor works with people can, and frequently does, affect significantly the people's careers, and indeed their lives. An approach based on prejudice, a decision based in ignorance, a careless remark based on indifference, can easily lead to injustice and, in certain settings, to disaster. As many scientists in the fields of sociology, psychology, and associated areas have pointed out, we have a long way to go before we have enough facts on which to base our understanding of each other. One day perhaps, supervisors will possess the sure knowledge enabling them to deal with their people in a fully enlightened way. In the meantime, supervisors everywhere owe it to their people, no less than to themselves, to keep informed of the best and most factual information available to help them deal reasonably with their associates.

Book Co., 1961), pp. 416–428; and "Notes on a General Theory of Administration," *Administrative Science Quarterly*, June 1956, pp. 1–29.

My studies of supervision and management and my experience with supervisors have led me to conclude that there is little significant difference between supervision in government agencies, businesses, industries, and other organizations.[2] This appears to be true both in the United States and in at least fifty other countries with whose representatives I have had opportunities to work. Problems with human beings at work are basically similar no matter where they occur. In the area of human relations, supervisors of whatever "level," or status, or salary, or title, or national origin, or skin color, or sex, seem to be faced with common problems. In all my hundreds of groups, with any mixture of supervisors, I have never experienced a situation in which the supervisors had difficulty understanding each other's problems. Variations in human nature seem to be as great between any two individual supervisors as between groups of supervisors from different kinds of organizations, "levels," or countries.

The nature of human beings is such that human uniqueness and similarity are distributed worldwide. It is not different because of culture, institutions, or religion. Human nature is much more fundamental in character than any of these distinctions. I suggest that it is about time we learned and took seriously what the great religious leaders, philosophers, educators, and thinkers have been telling us for centuries upon centuries. How shall we, indeed, deal with our fellow man?

More than twenty years have elapsed since the first edition of this book was published in 1962. During that period there have been some truly tremendous developments in the field of supervision. This is particularly true of the last half dozen years, when a number of books and articles have appeared dealing with managerial and supervisory methods used in Japan. I have been considering these for a number of years,

2. Harvey Sherman has also expressed this idea in his book *It All Depends*, (University of Alabama Press, 1966).

indeed, and first wrote about them in 1974 in *The Successful Manager.*

It is now clear that Japan has in general far surpassed the United States in the skill with which Japanese supervisors work with the people they supervise. I have dealt with this in the chapter on productivity. Ironically enough, many of their approaches are based importantly on research performed in the United States, as many Japanese have freely admitted.

In the United States we are still *talking* about the ideas and making tentative steps at implementing them; the Japanese have long since put them in action. In the meantime, the works of Likert, Herzberg, Marrow, and many others set forth in the first edition of this book, remain of cardinal importance in supervision. The Japanese have found their improved supervision to be important not only in Japan itself but also in the organizations they manage in the United States as well as elsewhere.

The section on performance review speaks for itself. I am much indebted to one of my students, Merlyn Meyen, for this material. He developed it at the University of Arizona Extension Winter School in 1980. He very generously gave permission to use it in this edition of the book.

W. R. V.
August 1985

1

Some Preliminary Ideas

There are few jobs more difficult but at the same time more interesting than that of supervising people. It takes more skill, more common sense, more imagination, more good humor, and certainly as much intelligence as any other kind of work. And it can frequently hold more grief, more trouble, and more difficulties than other kinds of work, particularly for the man or woman who has not learned the art of working with other people.

Most people who work were employed in the first place not because they could supervise but because they had some other skill or knowledge needed to perform a job. People enter the government service as they enter business or industry, first of all because they are willing to work—a qualification of basic importance (though we sometimes take it for granted). They may be unskilled, in which case their willingness to work is possibly all they have to offer. They may be skilled, in which case they come to their jobs as carpenters, typists, stenographers, mechanics, laboratory technicians, or some other kind of skilled worker. Many others come to their jobs well-trained in accounting, engineering, biology, forestry, law, chemistry, physics, or in other scientific or professional fields, and most of them go through four or more years of college or university training. Few are employed originally as supervisors.

Some of the people who do a good job—skilled, unskilled, or professional—are eventually put in charge of a group of other people and designated as supervisors.

This is a major change. The new supervisor cannot rely on the skill or knowledge of former work to help solve the many new problems facing him or her. No matter how skilled a mechanic, no matter how good an accountant, no matter how knowledgeable in law or science, they are not therefore automatically able to supervise people. They encounter difficult and stubborn problems in human relations, communications, and management. These do not yield to manual dexterity or to the principles of the sciences or professions in which they might have been trained. They must fall back on what they know from general experience in order to solve problems that may often prove to be of great complexity and difficulty. This, in a thousand variations, is what has happened to supervisors almost everywhere.

When new supervisors begin to realize their own deficiencies—and there are some who never do, of course—they may do one of several things. They may request a transfer to their old work and thank heaven to be back among familiar things. Or they may rock along as best they can on what little they know or think they know. Or they may systematically go about the task of equipping themselves to operate as skillfully as they are able in the new field of supervision.

In this illustration—endlessly repeated in agencies and organizations of every description—it is clear that people cannot divorce themselves entirely from the work situation out of which they were promoted. Nor should they try. Actually, supervisors usually continue to work in much the same environment as before. They continue to work with people who are doing the same kind of work that they were doing before. What they do as supervisors, however, is now different from what they used to do as one of the workers. The contribution they are now expected to make to the work of the organization requires knowledge and ability that they may have exercised only to a limited degree, if at all, in former jobs.

In fact, a person who has become a supervisor has entered what has been recognized for some time as a professional field of its own. In this field there exists a large body of knowledge that a supervisor must know and understand. Many competent people have written about the subject matter involved. There is, indeed, an enormous library of material, which is growing rapidly as new developments continue. It is true that those with scientific training may consider supervision and management to be less scientific in character than is chemistry, or physics, or the other exact sciences. And they would be right. It is a field in which the results are much more difficult to predict. But this need not detract from the progress already made, nor does it invalidate the painfully learned lessons of experience. It would, indeed, be well if more scientists were in this field, for they might bring to it the kind of thinking and the method of approach familiar in their own disciplines.

At any rate, new supervisors who realize their need for development in the professional field of supervision can help themselves in a number of ways. As they go about this, let them realize that they are not alone! By far the majority of supervisors have had to do it, and the chances are reasonably good that new ones can do it too. Here are some of the ways:

1. Many books have been written about supervision, human relations, executive development, management, administration, and related subjects. Any supervisor ought to know the best books in this field, and it would be well to get together at least a small personal library of his or her own. If these books can be read critically, testing what they say against experience, much of value can be derived from them. Chapter 16 tells about some of these books and indicates which may be helpful in this endeavor.

2. A number of professional journals and magazines contain new ideas and new developments in the field of supervision and management. Some of these are listed in Chapter

16. Most of these journals can be borrowed from a library, and a supervisor can get the one or two that he or she comes to value most by subscribing to them. This usually means joining a professional society, and this, too, is a useful thing to do. At the periodic meetings of such societies a supervisor can meet other people engaged in the same kind of work. Ideas and techniques can be exchanged with them and new points of view about the toughest problems can be obtained.

3. There is always, of course, the possibility of enrolling in courses offered by colleges and universities in one phase or another of supervisory work. There are night courses, short courses, special workshops or conferences, and home study courses. They, like books, can help a supervisor learn although they cannot solve all problems. Supervisors sincerely trying to improve themselves can use another way. They can review and analyze, as objectively as possible, the way in which they are working and getting results. Many people find this procedure difficult to follow. It comes more easily with experience, possibly because a more mature mind can acknowledge mistakes more readily. Self-analysis is never easy, because most of us habitually try to excuse or rationalize what we have done. Rather than admit even to themselves that they were in error, new supervisors are likely to use this self-appraisal primarily to convince themselves that they were basically right in whatever they did. Of course, the question is not whether they were right or wrong, but whether they were successful in getting one or all of the supervised people to perform correctly and productively.

At any rate, the critical and thoughtful review of his or her own work by a supervisor can provide a guide toward better ways of operating. If they can be as critical of themselves as they are of other people, if they can clearly imagine themselves in the position of others, then what they may conclude can often prove of great value in future work. Sometimes one's wife or husband, a close friend (*not* in the supervisor's unit), another supervisor, can help with this appraisal. But the need for evaluation of one's own performance is clear. The results are far superior to experience alone; they are evaluated experience.

Kinds of Supervision and Supervisors

Many years ago I accidentally stumbled on a teaching device in a group where our discussions about supervision were having heavy going. Too many of the people in the class seemed to have a deep-seated resentment about supervisors as they had known them. In some desperation I stopped the discussion and suggested we make a list of examples of poor supervisory practice. The items flooded forth so fast it was scarcely possible to get them written on the blackboard. When I began to challenge an occasional idea, interesting and useful discussions resulted.

The aftermath was curious. After the discussion, in which feelings sometimes ran high, the group temper changed. As if eager to compensate for their expressed resentment, the participants became constructive. They worked hard at explaining and discussing what they thought good supervision ought to be. Since then, I have begun many conferences or classes on supervision with the same device. It is easy to get people to say what they *do not* like about supervision. They let off a good bit of steam; they seem to like to do it; and unfortunately nearly all seem to have plenty of examples to offer out of their own experience. The lists always tend to include many examples of poor supervisors; that is, there is a tendency to personalize. The items do not come in any particular order, but the lists look something like this:

1. Loud reprimanding in the presence of other people.
2. Favoritism toward certain individuals in the unit.
3. Insufficient knowledge of the work.
4. Poor instruction—either too general or not complete.
5. Deadlines not explained in advance.

6. Use of employees as scapegoats for the supervisor's errors.

7. Refusal to admit mistakes.

8. Failure to support (and fight for) people under them.

9. "Picky"—finds fault with everything the people do.

10. "Snoopervision"—always poking his or her nose into personal matters (usually explained as different from being *asked* for advice on personal matters).

11. Oversupervision—that is, too close watching of everything the people are doing.

12. Failure to delegate authority where needed.

13. Lack of full trust.

14. Habit of gossiping about one of the people with another in the same group.

15. Failure to give credit where credit is due.

16. Failure to provide adequate materials or facilities for the people supervised.

17. Inability to get clear-cut, prompt decisions.

18. Treatment of his or her people as inferiors, not as associates.

19. Display of too much "brass"; never lets anyone forget who is the boss.

20. Reluctance to give people a chance (i.e., to get credit, to win promotions, to use their own initiative, etc.).

Some lists have run to as many as fifty to seventy-five items, with surprisingly little duplication. Actually, it is rare for a group of a dozen or more adults to list as few as the twenty items above. On the other hand, every one of the twenty occurs in almost every list.

Such lists as these have been published before,[1] but they are possibly of greatest value when placed where they may easily be seen every day by the supervisor who helped make

---

1. For example, see Edward C. Kellogg, "The Top-Flight Supervisor: A Profile" in *Leadership on the Job—Guides to Good Supervision,* ed. Supervisory Management Staff of the American Management Association (New York, 1957), pp. 18–25.

one. After all, these are examples of things to be avoided. It is by such things that people judge their supervisors. And any set of principles purporting to be basic to supervision must take such examples as these into account.

We could at this point attempt to classify supervisors into a number of categories, although no useful purpose is served by doing so. It is worth our while, however, to distinguish between an autocratic leader and a democratic leader.[2] The autocrat we often call a "boss," which derives from the Dutch *baas,* meaning master. The *baas* is the one who directs, commands, and controls the people over whom authority is exercised in such a way that no one ever forgets who is indeed the *baas.* Such a boss frequently drives the people, using authority much like a whip, demanding complete obedience from "inferiors," and to a greater or lesser degree acts as a petty tyrant. This type believes that all the people have to do is what they are told. In spite of dissatisfaction and hard feelings among the people, he or she is often able to get good production out of the group, although there is ample evidence to indicate that this production is not as great as can be had by less authoritarian means.[3]

Conversely, a democratic leader is one who uses little authority; who encourages the people to participate in getting the job done; who deals fairly and patiently with the people and with good humor; who treats people as associates in a joint undertaking; and who obviously likes and is respected by the members of the group. Such a man or woman is seldom referred to as the "boss," except in a respectfully friendly way. We are inclined to think of him or her as a

2. Auren Uris has written an excellent article on this subject, which was reprinted in *Readings in Management,* eds. Max D. Richards and William A. Nielander (Cincinnati: South-Western, 1958), pp. 377–385.

3. Rensis Likert, Director of the Institute for Social Research at the University of Michigan, has summarized a good deal of data on this point in "Developing Patterns in Management," American Management Association General Management Series 178: 32–51, 1955, and 182: 3–29, 1956. See also his book *The Human Organization: Its Management and Value* (New York: McGraw-Hill, 1967).

leader in the truest sense. Commonly, a democratic leader is successful in encouraging the people to exert the greatest and most intelligent efforts of which they may be capable. As with the boss's group, he or she experiences dissatisfactions, but they are seldom bitter. It is a privilege and a pleasure to work with such supervisors. Some of them are great in the same sense that some teachers are great.

A number of different terms are used to designate supervisors. For example, a "manager" is a person who directs the work of an organization or a segment of it. Inevitably, he or she is a supervisor, since the work of any organization is performed by people and direction must flow through them. Administrators, executives, and directors are all supervisors, since their operations must always be carried out by other people. Foremen, of course, are supervisors. So is a "chief," a word much used in government to specify the head of a bureau, division, or branch. Terms such as these carry with them some additional ideas. People often associate mahogany desks and thick carpets with the term "executive." A foreman is often thought of as a supervisor in an industrial plant, or of unskilled labor, and so on.

Because these terms are in common use, many people tend to think that they have precise meanings and that everyone uses them to mean the same thing. This is simply not the case. All these terms have meanings that overlap a good deal, even though some books or authorities try to give them special meanings for special purposes.

What Supervisors Must Be Able to Do

Anyone working as a supervisor of people and a manager of work must learn how to do a number of things. We can list these as follows:

1. Learn how to guide and direct the efforts of the people being supervised. This involves learning about the many factors that motivate people, and understanding and using

skillfully the principles and methods of supervision known to be effective. Chapters 2 through 7 deal with this subject.

✓ 2. Learn how to work in the organization of which the people being supervised are a part. This implies that a supervisor must know something about the principles of organization and how an organization operates most efficiently. We treat this in Chapter 12.

3. Learn how to train or teach people to do their jobs. The supervisor must be able to train people for jobs of greater responsibility. There is a discussion of this in Chapter 10.

4. Learn how to speak and write clearly and effectively, and how to read and listen. There are techniques for doing all these, and they are often lumped under the term "communications." This comes in Chapter 11.

5. Learn how to analyze work loads. Anyone trying to supervise people and manage resources has to be able to judge what a fair day's work is—or a week's work, or a year's work. If this can be done, it is easier to judge whether one is overstaffed or understaffed. In addition, the supervisor needs to know how the various kinds of work should be assigned. This helps the supervisor to avoid using high-priced people on low-priced work, or the reverse. We come to this in Chapter 14.

6. Learn how to make a plan of action or operation. Good planning is important in any job, but particularly so in management. Chapter 14 considers this.

7. Learn how to schedule work, making a timetable for a plan and assigning priorities to the various jobs involved in it. This, too, is treated in Chapter 14, since a plan without a timetable is not really complete.

✓ 8. Learn how to improve operating efficiency. This is the kind of thing that pays off in easier, less costly operation. The methods are discussed in Chapter 14.

Chapter 15 considers ways to solve problem cases. Chapter 16 deals with important books and magazines in the field of supervision and management.

2

Basic Principles of Supervision

Supervision is the art of working with a group of people over whom authority is exercised in such a way as to achieve their greatest combined effectiveness in getting work done. It is best performed in an atmosphere of goodwill and zestful cooperation on the part of all the people involved—including, of course, the supervisor. It is possibly one of the most difficult of all the arts, since it demands an ability to use successfully and almost intuitively those principles of human relations that have proved true with most people most of the time.

Experienced supervisors will recognize that there are no sure and certain rules for working with "people" in general. They know, with the wisdom born of experience, that human beings are individually unique, and that this individuality must always be considered in developing working relations. With due regard for the uniqueness of individuals, however, there are certain general principles that are used by successful supervisors as guides in working with their people. Each principle involves some companion ideas that must be understood in order to appreciate the guiding principle. These principles are set forth below, with a discussion of each. The order in which they are listed is not significant; all of them are important.

PRINCIPLE ONE
> *People must always understand clearly what is expected of them.*

Ordinarily, when people start new work, they are eager to know what sort of an outfit they are getting into and what they are supposed to do, that is, what their particular job is going to be. An experienced supervisor takes advantage of this initial interest. Such supervisors know that if they fail to get a new person off to a good start, it may take more time and harder work to do it later on. They also know that possibly never again will the new worker be as receptive and eager to learn as in the very beginning. At any rate, every new person should find out *very soon* after reporting for work:

1. What the organization stands for; how it is organized; how it operates; what it does; something of its history; and the career policy it uses with its personnel.

Getting these ideas across is essentially an exercise in salesmanship. The intent here is to convince the new workers that they have entered the best possible organization, containing the finest people, doing the most important work in the most enlightened and efficient way. People like to feel that their outfit is a good one. They will put their best efforts into something important. Pride of organization is a motivating force with many people. Belief in the importance of what their organization does lends prestige to their part in it.

2. What a particular job is; how a job is related to those of fellow workers; what authority, if any, the job carries; and who the supervisor is.

It is with this group of items that there is often a good deal of confusion, sometimes for many years. Even if a new person is started off correctly, it is important to review these items from time to time. In a way, almost everything a worker does later on depends on knowing who is the boss and having a clear-cut understanding of what the job is and how it fits with related jobs.

3. Where to get needed materials, supplies, or equipment; where the place of work is; and what the working rules of the organization are. These last would include such things as payday; time of starting and quitting work; taking coffee breaks, lunch period, and leave; and all the other various rules peculiar to a particular organization.

Possibly, these things go without saying. These are important; they should be given attention. Here the supervisor may not need to explain personally. Other workers can— and will.

4. How the quality of the work will be measured.

5. How the quantity of the work will be measured.

Both items 4 and 5 need careful thought. It is discouraging indeed for people to find out after they have been working for some time that the quality of their work is below par. It is equally discouraging to learn too late that they are not producing as much as the supervisor expected. Quality and quantity must be understood *in advance*. Unless they are, there is likely to be argument about them when individuals discover they do not see eye to eye with their supervisor on either or both items.

There are, possibly, other things a supervisor would need to be sure the people know. For example, in certain government agencies and, indeed, certain industries, a new person has to learn about security rules if the work involves secret materials or activities. In any event, all such things require discussion between the supervisor and the new person. This discussion had better be planned for in a systematic way. If it is not, some items are bound to be overlooked or forgotten. This will not be the fault of the new person.

A good deal of the information a new person needs should be in written form. Many government agencies—but not all—have such things as these in writing, and so do some industries and businesses:

An organization chart.

The objectives and operating policies of the organization.

The history of the agency.

The career system the agency uses.

General office rules for all personnel.

Individual job descriptions and explanations.

Performance standards of quantity and quality.

Individual training outlines for each job.

Armed with a full set of materials like these, a supervisor can do a much better and more complete job than if he or she has to remember it all. Organizations that are aware that people are their most important asset will have these items prepared and available. Some organizations put the first five items in an employee's handbook or orientation manual. Obviously, the last three items are individual in character.

PRINCIPLE TWO
People must have guidance in doing their work.

Guidance is a general word. To be specific, it includes such things as these:

1. *Current information.* No one should be expected to work in the dark. Everyone wants to know what is going on that may affect the work. It is up to the supervisor to see that new developments—things about to happen, things that have taken place—are fully and promptly told to all the members of his group. This can be done in meetings or staff conferences, that is, with all of the people at the same time. If the job is done with one of the people at a time, it takes much longer, and the chances are that the grapevine will take over. News often gets twisted and distorted on the grapevine. The consequences of listening to wrong or partially wrong information can often be troublesome or even disastrous. A grapevine has its roots in poor supervisory practice; it flourishes best where supervisors are careless about keeping their people up to date.

2. *Specialty information.* In addition to news about developments, people must see and study the latest and best technical or special information relating to their work. The latest theories, principles, materials, and knowledge concerning their particular specialties are important to any worker. This may seem to be overgeneralized for every kind of worker. Possibly, unskilled laborers could get along without such information, but a better shovel, a better way to dig a ditch, a better broom or machine for cleaning floors, better equipment for moving heavy objects, better know-how in any kind of work whatever—all such things may help to improve the productivity of the people and their interest in the work.

In the professional fields, it is obvious that no forester or engineer, no physicist, no doctor, lawyer, or economist, no specialist in any field can develop without study of new knowledge in his field. It may be true, of course, that supervisors cannot personally provide all such information; in fact, it would be better if they did not try. But they have a responsibility for seeing that such knowledge is readily accessible and easily available; for studying their people to ascertain where each is strong and where weak; for encouraging and promoting study of the right kind. Principle Six considers this last point more completely.

3. *Information on techniques.* Techniques vary with the kind of job, and thoughtful supervisors will do well to make a checklist for each job in their unit. They must be sure that each of their people knows the best *methods* for getting the particular work done. Methods or techniques are somewhat different from knowledge about the work, although they tend to merge.

But there are often techniques that are by no means part of the special knowledge needed to perform a given job. For example, many professional people do not always know such things as these:

a. How to listen.
b. How to speak.
c. How to write.
d. How to read.
e. How to organize work.
f. How to schedule activities.
g. How to conduct a meeting.

There are many how-to-do-it items that can be listed for any particular job, and there are some, such as the first six above, common to many jobs. The point is that supervisors must be alert to the necessity of helping people to use the easiest and most efficient techniques known. They should not only be on the lookout for these better techniques, but they should be working with their people in a systematic way to develop them. (See Chapter 11 about this.)

4. *Personality improvement.* The last of our guidance items is perhaps the most difficult to effect. Making personality improvement suggestions requires skillful handling. Every human being *has* shortcomings, and almost everyone will admit that he or she is not perfect. But point out to a particular individual that he or she has a particular fault—and you may be in trouble. Frequently, the person will deny the charge with some heat, although sometimes he or she will surprise you by admitting it. He or she may be lazy, or slow, or too talkative, or moody, or short-tempered, or too hasty in making decisions, or what have you. The trouble frequently is that such individuals may not admit it, even to themselves. And yet, all employees are entitled to help from their supervisor on their weak personality points.

A thoughtful supervisor sees to it that each person receives helpful encouragement—by one means or another—to overcome a personality fault that may stand in the way of full expression of ability. I know of no successful formula for providing this encouragement or guidance and for getting it accepted. Success seems to rest on (a) recognition by the person of the fault, (b) prevention of too great discouragement about it, (c) development of a real desire to overcome it, and (d) constructive help and encouragement in conquering it.

Each of these points is important. Generally recognition of the fault by the person is the most difficult to achieve. Too hard pressure on this first point may make the discouragement almost a disaster when the recognition finally comes. Too great discouragement makes for difficulty in developing a desire to overcome the fault. Once these steps are taken, help in conquering the fault is much easier to give and more certain to be accepted. This is possibly similar to the method described by Alcoholics Anonymous to make a nonalcoholic out of an alcoholic. There is no question but that the method is successful more often than not; however, as the AA people describe it, their method depends on the acknowledgment or recognition or confession of weakness, without which there is little hope for progress. The technique of correction is worth close study, particularly in more difficult cases.

PRINCIPLE THREE
Good work should always be recognized.

Almost any experienced supervisor will agree readily enough that this is a good principle. Such recognition should be as public as possible. People like to feel appreciated, and they will work all the harder when their efforts are noticed and commended. But supervisors will also tell you, almost in the same breath, that this can easily be overdone. The worst part of it is that fear of overdoing it frequently acts to prevent some supervisors from giving any praise at all.

Nevertheless, opinion surveys continue to indicate clearly and unmistakably that people consider recognition of good work a characteristic of good supervisors. They consider lack of ready recognition of good work characteristic of poor supervision. The question is: What is the best way to put this principle into effective, reasonable operation?

Listed below are some of the ways supervisors can recognize the good work that many of their people perform. They are arranged in order, beginning with the simplest and easiest way of all:

1. *Tell* individuals, on the spot, that they have just done a good job. Do this preferably in the presence of other people.

2. *Write* to them, promptly and explicitly, and see that a copy of the letter gets into their personnel folder. (Throughout the federal government, in many state governments, in many companies, and in some other organizations, a personnel file is maintained for each individual in the organization. Such files can be of immense value as a repository for all the actions and records concerning each of the people working in the company or agency. Generally these files, even after many years, contain few or no letters of commendation of the sort we are describing here.)

At this point let me note that telling individuals or writing to them costs little or nothing. These are the least expensive, but possibly most valuable, ways of according recognition. The items following contain the more expensive methods.

3. Give them a certificate of merit, of whatever type the organization uses—if it has one.

4. Give them a cash award or bonus.

5. Give them a medal or certificate plus a cash award.

6. Give them a raise.

7. Promote them to a better job for which they are qualified.

From this list it is obvious that the method of recognition must be tailored to the degree of excellence of performance and made in accordance with the policies of the organization.

But all this depends primarily on whether supervisors are intent on making the principle of recognition actually work.

It is not necessarily true that the more awards there are, the better the supervision. But it does seem clear that the easy, simple methods of telling people or writing to people about their good jobs well done are basic supervisory techniques.

PRINCIPLE FOUR
Poor work deserves constructive criticism.

If it is true that good work deserves recognition, it seems equally true that poor work must also be appropriately recognized. This is an area in which most of us excel. It seems, somehow, far easier to criticize than to praise. It often seems easier to detect poor work than to detect good work. And yet, all employees deserve (and usually expect) criticism of poor work that they have done (and that they recognize to be poor).

Criticism should be given in private. Public censure of a worker is compounded by the number of other people who see and hear the person receive it. But it is not enough to confine criticism to private sessions between the supervisor and one of the people. The criticism must also be constructive.

One of the best ways to lower employees' satisfaction with their work, their interest in the job, and even their self-confidence, is to bawl them out. A good bawling-out may relieve a supervisor's feelings about a mistake or a poor job, and it may satisfy the supervisor's ego, but it will most certainly not improve the productivity of the unit. Workers who have been harshly criticized or unmercifully tongue-lashed may seethe for months over the incident. They may not get over it for a long time, possibly for years. Their resentment may well find expression in doing less than they could do if they felt like it. Here again, opinion surveys among government as well as industrial workers show clearly that people simply do not consider supervisors top-ranking who are unnecessarily harsh in dealing with their people.

The supervisors' objective is to keep their people operating at their fullest possible capacity. When they do poor work, their task is to get them to do better, not to vent their dissatisfactions on them. The question is not who is to blame, but always how to improve their people's efforts.

PRINCIPLE FIVE
People should have opportunities to show that they can accept greater responsibilities.

Sooner or later every job in any organization will become vacant, and a new person will have to be put in it. The "head-scratching" method of filling an unexpected vacancy is a poor one. In contrast, any agency led by people of vision seeks to be ready to fill any and all vacancies whenever they occur. This requires that all supervisors take advantage of every opportunity to let their people show what they can do. When the time comes for filling a vacancy, there is no need for uncertainty or head-scratching. The best people are already known, because they have been trained and tried. The only problem is to choose the best qualified. We are assuming here, of course, that simple seniority is not the criterion for promotion but that the best-qualified people, regardless of age or sex or color, are given the opportunity to advance.

The grooming of people for positions of greater responsibility takes record-keeping. When individuals have a chance to show what they can do, a good supervisor duly makes a note of how well they performed, and files it in the personnel folder. The opportunities include special assignments to more difficult work or to other locations or offices. Supervisors' field trips or vacations provide other opportunities to leave others in charge. The whole point is to *plan* on developing people. Incidentally, individuals who work steadily at their own improvement are more likely to bloom when they have the chance. This, too, a good supervisor encourages and carefully notes.

Testing people before a full-fledged vacancy occurs is one way to avoid poor placement. It is not a positive guarantee, of course, because people change, but it does help materially to cut down the numbers of poor transfers or promotions. Putting untried people in jobs is not good management. And supervisors who believe they have an unfailing ability to pick good workers are due for some surprises.

So far, all of this is from the point of view of the organization and the supervisor. From the point of view of the people involved (and *all* of us in an organization are involved), the opportunity for advancement is one of the things they work for. Students fresh out of college always want to know what kind of career an agency can offer and what their opportunities are likely to be. No use telling them, "When I was your age, I was glad just to have a job." This is the land of opportunity; young people charting their course want to know where they are likely to be in five or ten years or more.

Futhermore, when they perform successfully in one job, they know as well as their supervisor does, and as well as their agency or company should, that they deserve an opportunity in a more responsible job. They want—and may well deserve—more responsibility, higher salary, improved status.

Both from the standpoint of the organization and of the employees, then, a supervisor is well advised to take advantage of or create opportunities for his or her people to get ahead. Parenthetically, let me note that a supervisor who comes to be recognized as a developer of good workers is likely to find advancement more rapid.

PRINCIPLE SIX
People should be encouraged to improve themselves.

For many years in America there has been all too common acceptance of the erroneous idea that when students graduate from school, they are "educated." Whether from grammar school, high school, college, or university makes little difference except in degree. Your diploma becomes your passport, although it is recognized that college diplomas will get you into more places than will high school diplomas. In a sense, these diplomas have come to be regarded as certificates of separation—of separation from all further education.

Such ideas have led Robert Blakeley to characterize American education as *terminal* in character.[1] As he sees it, "you are educated only if you ceaselessly continue to educate yourself"—a statement he once made to a college graduating class. And with such an idea, educators, scientists, people of affairs, leaders in professional fields, and well-educated people everywhere agree most heartily.

For eight, twelve, sixteen, or more years individuals may receive intensive training in various subjects. The intent, generally, is to show them how to use their mental faculties for solving various kinds of problems. Most of the problems they deal with in school are simulated or borrowed; they are not necessarily real, nor are they necessarily the person's own. When they leave school, they begin to encounter problems in great variety, never considered or discussed in school. Generally, the more education they have had, the better equipped they may be to deal successfully with these new problems.

To most Americans, education almost always conjures up visions of a school building and classrooms. People speak of education as though it were a sort of commodity that is to be had if one goes to get it at the proper place. As Blakeley puts it, this kind of thinking enables us to say to each other: "I got my education at Podunk. Where'd you get yours?" In fact, our education is never finished, not until our lives end. There

1. In *Adult Education in a Free Society,* a collection of speeches, ed. J. R. Kidd (Toronto, Canada: Guardian Bird Publications, 1958).

is nothing for it; either we continue our education and, thereby, our ability to solve new problems or we stagnate. There is no middle course.

People can improve their minds in many ways: by reading; by discussion, especially with people more able than themselves; by expressing themselves in writing; and in other ways. It is a wise supervisor who can so stimulate people that they continue to be eager to learn, thirsty for knowledge, and alert for new and useful ideas. To so stimulate people requires great skill and thoughtfulness; many teachers are unable to do this, at least with all their students. And yet we are suggesting that where trained and experienced teachers may have failed, nevertheless, supervisors should try very hard. Those who succeed will find they have a group of people working with them who are going places and who bring to their work such imagination and vision as may transform their daily tasks.

PRINCIPLE SEVEN
People should work in a safe and healthful environment.

The last of our "half-dozen" principles is this one, which is so often overlooked. Almost anyone will agree that this is a supervisory responsibility wherever, for example, the people in a unit make use of machinery or drive automotive equipment. There is recognition, too, of this responsibility where the people involved must do heavy physical work. But it is much less common to find supervisors who are well aware of the safety and health precautions necessary in an ordinary business office.

Any office has plenty of potential hazards. Tripping over light cords or open file drawers at the bottom of a cabinet; standing in front of doors that may be swung open unexpectedly; catching arms, hands, or legs on furniture edges or splinters; trying to move too-heavy furniture; slipping on waxed floors; finding electric fixtures in disrepair—all such simple situations can and do lead to serious accidents. Besides these, there are ventilation, lighting, and other problems in any enclosed work place that can become of major consequence. There are technical standards for these, all easily available from the National Safety Council. There are health hazards, too—for example, the overly conscientious worker who comes to the office with a severe and contagious cold—and these too require supervisory attention. Many people are not as fully aware of safety and health hazards as they should be. If a supervisor does not pay attention to this matter, who will?

3

Supervisor's Expectations

A few years ago a social psychologist and an education specialist conducted an unusual experiment in a California elementary school.[1] They had reason to believe from previous studies that children in school might do better *if their teachers expected them to.*

The experimenters got the teachers to give a special intelligence test to their more than five hundred students. This test was not a new one, but it was unfamiliar to the teachers. They were told that the test could reveal children who were about to spurt ahead in their studies, or "bloom" scholastically.

After the tests had been collected, however, they were simply filed away and not used at all. Instead, the names of 20 percent of the students in the school were picked at random—or essentially, as the report puts it, drawn out of a hat. Their names were specially marked on class lists, which were turned over to the teachers. These marked names, the teachers were told, indicated the children who had scored high on the special test. They were the students who were about to spurt or bloom.

All the children in the school had been previously classified into groups or tracks, as is done normally in many of our

1. Robert Rosenthal and Lenore Jacobson, *Pygmalion in the Classroom* (New York: Holt, 1968).

schools—a fast track, a medium track, and a slow track. But the names pulled out of the hat in the study were absolutely random, so that mixed in the sample were students from the slow, the medium, and the high tracks. There was, in fact, no relation whatever between the special intelligence test the children had taken and their ability. Actually, the only difference between the "special" children and their classmates was *in the minds of the teachers.*

Careful records were made of the children's IQs determined by usual tests both before the special test was administered and at intervals thereafter. The results were impressive and statistically significant. The children *not* on the earmarked list gained an average of more than eight IQ points, but the children on the lists as bloomers gained more than twelve points. In other words, the selected children did 50 percent better than did the unselected ones. And because their teachers expected them to spurt ahead, this is exactly what they did.

We should note here that other studies have shown that it is very difficult to increase IQ scores even with the most concentrated coaching. In the experiments described above, both the control group (unmarked) and the experimental group (the designated or marked children) increased their IQ scores significantly. The biggest improvements, though, were in the experimental group of children, and the conclusion is clear that the children did better if their teachers expected them to. This is what our two researchers had set out to check.

It is also interesting to note that the biggest gains were made by children in the first and second grades. In these grades one out of five undesignated children gained twenty IQ points or more, but of the special children, one out of two gained that much. There were other highly interesting results in this *Pygmalion in the Classroom* study. One was that the effects of teacher expectation began to show up within only a few weeks. Another was that the effects lasted afterward for periods ranging from a number of months up to nearly two years.

The experimenters did not know how the teachers may have communicated their expectations to the children, but they believe that this must have been a matter of attitude. By the tone of voice, by the way the teachers looked at them, the children may have deduced the degree of teachers' confidence or expectation of them. Teachers may have paid greater attention to the selected children and have been more pleasant, friendly, encouraging. Of course such attitudes also rub off on others—the unselected children—which would help explain the gains in IQ that they made as well.

Rosenthal and Jacobson summarize numerous other studies that point in the same direction as their study. We may especially note one of these, performed by A. Bavelas. In his experiments foremen were led to believe that some of the women under their supervision had scored high on tests of intelligence and finger dexterity when actually they had gotten low scores. The foremen were told that others had scored low, when they really had scored high. The foremen did not know which women had scored high and which low, but *they thought they did.* In other words, the foremen, like the teachers, were deceived. Regardless of the high or low scores, however, if the foremen expected high performance, the production record of the women workers proved superior to that of other workers. And where the foremen expected low performance, they got just that.

A study by Gordon and Durea is cited in which "when examiners behaved more warmly toward their eighth-grade subjects, the IQ scores obtained were over six points higher than when they behaved more coolly toward their adolescent subjects."

They cite Crow, who found that college-age subjects performed better at a coding task if they were treated warmly. In other experiments, military personnel were more alert in detecting signals "when the experimenter was warmer, and less alert when the experimenter was cooler toward the subjects." And more warmly treated nursery school children scored nearly ten IQ points higher than did children who were treated with indifference. Other citations from the literature caused Rosenthal and Jacobson to conclude that "at least sometimes a subject's performance of an intellectual task may be unintentionally determined by the prophecy (or expectation) of the examiner."[2]

In recent years mounting evidence shows that where and when children are expected by their teachers to perform in a superior way, the children will do so, regardless of IQ and other tests that indicate that they will not or cannot. Conversely, if teachers expect children to respond in an inferior way, the children respond in that way, again regardless of other tests predicting better performance.

Altogether, the work may be summarized by the sentence that opens *Pygmalion in the Classroom:* "People, more often than not, do what is expected of them."

What Supervisors Can Expect

There are many constraints and misconceptions that operate to defeat supervisors. Possibly foremost among these is the business of *classifying people,* a common habit among us all. Everyone tends to put people in compartments or categories. We decide that a person is either bright and even brilliant, or else dull or outright stupid. The person has talent, is "gifted," or has little or no talent. We carry this classifying into the classroom, as we have already seen, grouping stu-

2. In addition to the studies of Rosenthal and Jacobson, the interested student will find it well worthwhile to read "Managing Motivated Employees" by W. N. Penzer of IBM in *Personnel Journal*, May 1971; also J. Sterling Livingston, "Pygmalion in Management," *Harvard Business Review*, July–August 1969; and David E. Berlew and Douglas T. Hall, "The Socialization of Managers: Effects of Expectations on Performance," *Administrative Science Quarterly*, September 1966.

dents into fast, medium, and slow tracks. In college we may put them into A, B, C, D groups, or failures.

Most such classifications as these are supposed to relate directly to intelligence or brain power. But we also place people in fast, medium, or slow groupings for other reasons. The assumption is often made that a person with a skin color other than white may prove to be less intelligent or possessed of less ability. Poorly dressed, unclean humans are often automatically classed in the slow track. Many studies by sociologists and psychologists have produced just such findings as these.

Scientific evidence indicates that we are often quite wrong in our assumptions and classifications. Besides the evidence coming from the work of Rosenthal, Jacobson, and many others, another important factor is often overlooked.

The fact is that every human being regardless of race, color, or sex receives at birth a human brain. This brain develops rapidly in the first few years of life. It is the most remarkable biological mechanism in existence. Our ability to perceive, to think, to reason, to learn, and to remember is built into the human nervous system with its ultimate directing center, the brain. This system is under genetic control; that is, human beings are *born* with an inherent capacity unmatched in any other organism.

The capacity of the human brain is fantastic. It contains more than a million million cells (or a trillion, or 10^{12} cells, if you like). The interconnections between these million million cells are more numerous than are the cells themselves. We have no actual idea yet how many cells and connections are involved in purely ordinary thoughts. We do know, though, that the brain we have is underutilized even by the most "brilliant" of humans. In an instant the brain can accept all the things that can be seen, felt, heard, smelled, or tasted, either individually or in any combination. It can evaluate these sensations or groups of sensations, decide upon those most likely to be prevailing, select with precision the motor units of the body that must thereupon be activated, and then control and regulate the resulting required actions both quantitatively and qualitatively. The number and complexity of computations required to do this "ordinary" sort of thing is staggering. Compared with the human brain, our most highly sophisticated computers are scarcely more than toys.[3]

The human brain can store enormous numbers of facts and ideas. It can reproduce these in any combination instantly or after a long period of years. It can arrange an infinite number of combinations of facts and ideas, evaluate them, compare them with stored standards, and issue orally or in other ways the possible conclusions resulting from such study. It can do this at once, in a little while, or after a long time.

And *every normal, ordinary human being anywhere in the world can do this.* The most creative, imaginative, innovative, intelligent creatures on the face of the earth are the human beings—black, white, red, yellow, or brown—that inhabit it.

The capacity of the human brain is still far beyond the understanding of our foremost scientists. We have done little more than tinker with it. The more it is studied, the more the brain defeats our analysis. There are major segments of the brain whose functions are completely unknown. The pathways of thought astound us with their complexity. The crude studies of what happens when part of the brain is destroyed come nowhere near explaining what happens inside the brain with respect to ordinary perception, evaluation, judgment, and memory. The study of its operation is beset with technical difficulties that we are only beginning to resolve. It is not the brain of the so-called genius we are talking about

3. A more complete summary of our existing knowledge about the human brain is presented in *Biology and the Future of Man,* edited by Philip Handler, president of the National Academy of Sciences (New York: Oxford, 1970), pp. 324–378. See also Carl Sagan, *The Dragon's of Eden* (New York: Ballantine, 1977).

here; it is every brain, the brain possessed by every normal human being.

What we are getting at here is the simple idea that instead of classifying human beings who possess this amazing brain, we had better address ourselves to methods aimed at getting it into full use. Instead of deciding in advance that any human being is slow, dull, stupid, or lacking in intelligence, let us take advantage of the remarkable power conferred on the person by his or her inherited capacity for thought.

This thought leads us back to the idea expressed in the beginning of this chapter. What we expect of other people, we are likely to receive—without any particular limit as far as we know, since all humans possess what appears to be an infinite capacity—the human brain.

Supervisory Approach

With the foregoing ideas in mind, let us now consider how they may be applied to the situation of supervisors with people under their direction. How can they use these ideas? Two major aspects of the matter are (1) clear awareness of the immense capacity of every human brain, and (2) expectation.

Interestingly, there is some highly important factual evidence concerning the results that can be attained through the application of these ideas. We turn, for example, to another field entirely, the work of the extraordinary Japanese violin teacher Shinichi Suzuki.[4]

Suzuki has taught the violin for more than thirty years. One day early in his career a father came into his studio with his four-year-old boy and asked Suzuki to teach the child to play the violin. Suzuki was uncertain; the child was too young; Suzuki had never worked with a small child before and

---

4. Shinichi Suzuki, *Nurtured by Love: A New Approach to Education* (New York: Exposition, 1969).

was not at all sure that it could be done. But he agreed to consider the matter.

Suzuki says in his book that as he thought about the problem, it dawned on him that this little boy could, after all, speak Japanese. And Japanese, no less than any other language, is a difficult thing to learn. If the little boy could learn Japanese at this young age, surely he could learn other "difficult" things, such as to play the violin. So Suzuki began trying to teach the boy and was successful.

He took on other youngsters. By now Suzuki has trained hundreds of thousands of children from four to ten years of age to play fine music on the violin. He says he has never had a single failure. None of his pupils had to pass a test before entering the school. And these children became what we call accomplished musicians. They play classical music written for the violin, and they play it well.

We may take the word of the great cellist Pablo Casals on the excellence of Suzuki's pupils. When Casals was in Tokyo he heard four hundred children, aged five to twelve, play their violins and was moved to tears by their skill.

Suzuki believed that any child has a virtually unlimited capacity, and he confidently expected each child to develop into an accomplished musician. And as he worked skillfully to develop the inherent talent he was sure was there, he succeeded.

Whether a student liked or disliked music or playing the violin is beside the point. All Japanese children don't necessarily like the Japanese language, but they learn it just the same. "Ability grows as it is trained," Suzuki says. If there are failures, it is the teacher who has failed, not the student. The time may come, the great teacher suggests, when not a single student will fail in school.

Of equal importance, Suzuki notes that "if you compare a person who practices five minutes a day with one who practices three hours a day, the difference—is enormous.

Those who fail to practice sufficiently fail to acquire ability.

"Superior ability," he goes on to say, "can be produced in anyone."

What can a supervisor do with such ideas? Are they practical? Bavelas' study with the foremen suggests that these ideas are indeed practical. But note that their usefulness depends on the sincere and honest belief of supervisors that all their people can prove to be outstanding employees. They cannot disguise their true feelings by hearty but insincere encouragement. The supervisors' underlying feelings, if they are negative, will inevitably be communicated to their people by an attitude that will give them away.

For such a reason, this discussion is somewhat detailed. Supervisors must understand the enormous capacity of the human brain—*any human brain*. They must know with certainty that the people under their supervision—fast, medium, or slow people—are alike in the capacity that they have for excellence. Supervisors must realize that their real problem is not to replace people with others classified as better or superior but rather to undertake the most skillful efforts of which they are capable to unleash and improve the abilities of the people they already have. They have before them the potential; it is up to them to help give it expression.

One last point must be made. Suzuki worked with children; so did Rosenthal and Jacobson. In the San Francisco school it was the youngest children who made the greatest gains. Suzuki, in fact, once turned down an offer to work in a new school dealing entirely with adults. He preferred not to do "repair work," as he said, but rather to work with relatively unspoiled youngsters. Are we to assume that it is too late to expect improvement in the adults with whom supervisors must ordinarily work?

It is by no means too late. Numerous studies have shown clearly enough that the responses of adults are quite similar to the responses of children. We have already noted Bavelas'

work with women, who were adults, and the experiments
with military personnel and college students. In the study of
corporation executives by Livingston, and of managers by
Berlew and Hall,[5] the men concerned were all adults. These
few studies are supported by many others. They may serve to
remind us of something Adlai Stevenson once said in the
United Nations Assembly. He remarked, "Children don't
grow older, they just grow taller."

But there is another aspect to the adult problem that is of
great importance. This is the fact that the first year in an organization is a very critical period for any new recruit. When
people enter a company or an agency for the first time, they
come into it much the same as children entered Suzuki's studio. Almost everything is new. If they are trained correctly
from the very beginning in this new situation, then little repair work is needed later on. "Never again will he [the new
person] be so . . . ready to learn as he is in his first year."[6]
The moral of all this is, then, for supervisors to undertake the
best training program they can devise, and to put it to work
with their new people from the very first day.

5. See Berlew and Hall's study, already cited on p. 27.
6. Ibid.

4

About Productivity

A few years ago something happened in America that attracted relatively little attention at the time. After almost two centuries of upward growth, the United States' *rate* of productivity began to slow down. It went downhill more and more rapidly. By 1973, only a half dozen years later, it was lower than that of Canada, lower than any one of the nine leading western European nations, including the United Kingdom, France, Germany, and Italy; and finally, lower than that of Japan. Actually the rate of productivity in Japan, Italy, Germany, and France surpassed that of the United States from 1950 to 1979, and the U.S. rate continues downward.

What all this means is that the American worker is producing less per hour than he or she did a year ago. As we are using the word here, and as it is generally defined, *productivity* is output per worker per hour, quality considered. The statement about productivity rate does not apply to farm workers; the United States' agricultural productivity rate continues to go up. But, except for the percent of the work force on farms, Americans are not doing as well as they should, or could, or once did.

Many economists feel that the growth rate of productivity is quite possibly the best single measure we have of the vitality of our economy. John Kendrick, a leading authority on the subject, has pointed out that the growth of productivity per worker was as follows:[1]

Period	Increase per year percent
1800–1855	0.5
1855–1890	1.1
1890–1919	2.0
1919–1948	2.4
1948–1966	3.2
1966–1973	2.1
1973–1979	0.8

Any number of reasons why our productivity rate has gone down have been offered. It is important that these reasons be carefully studied if we wish to be in a position to do something about improving the rate.

A relatively dramatic comparison of the rates of productivity increase for the top dozen countries from 1960 through 1973 shows the following:

United States	3.3 percent
Canada	4.3 percent
Western Europe	5.7 percent
(the nine leading industrial countries)	
Japan	10.7 percent

Although these figures are for 1960–1973, the rate of increase during 1973–1978 for Japan was nearly eight times as great as that of the United States. So was Germany's; and Canada's was twice as good. More recently, the figures for the United States have become smaller yet.

Such figures as these suggest, among other things, that it might pay to look at how organizations are managed in other developed countries, especially in Japan.

1. As set forth in "Better Prospects for Our Ailing Productivity," by William Bowen, *Fortune*, December 1979.

Management in Japan

In 1974, a report by two Stanford University professors entitled "Made in America (under Japanese management)" was published in the *Harvard Business Review*. It dealt with studies involving some twenty-two Japanese companies operating in the United States.[2]

The findings were quite clear. In general, the studies showed that Japanese companies were outproducing American companies in the same industries. Japanese workers were producing 15 percent more in Tokyo than were American workers in Atlanta—using the same number of workers, the same technology, and the same procedure in making the same transistor panels. But when Japanese managers were in charge of American workers, as they were in Sony's plant in San Diego, the American workers did as well in San Diego as did the Japanese workers in Tokyo. More recently, the American workers did even better than that.

The way the Japanese supervisors managed the workers—Japanese or American—somehow made a clear 15 percent difference. From this it seems obvious that the Japanese style of management may be quite usable in the United States. In other words, Americans could use the Japanese approach to improve their own productivity by as much as 15 percent, if not more.

I am well aware that statements such as the above have not been fully, if indeed at all, understood by most American managers. The tendency is to note the 15 percent improvement but to believe that this is owing simply to the Japanese culture. And the American managers may be partially correct, but only partially. In fact, much of the Japanese style can be used in America with little or no adaptation. Indeed, it has been used successfully long before this. As the Japa-

2. Richard T. Johnson and William E. Ouchi, *Harvard Business Review*, September-October 1974, pp. 61–69.

nese themselves have admitted, the research on which the Japanese management is based was performed in the United States.

We must note at this point that human beings the world around are first of all human beings; after that they may have different colors, histories, customs, and cultures. But as Stuart Chase once put it, "when you treat people as human beings, they respond as human beings." The Japanese have a well-developed philosophy about such an issue. They are concerned first about the employee and second about the product. In most American organizations the concern is first—and often wholly—about the product, a position that was clearly stated by an American manager in a Sony plant. He said, "You get a feeling around here that they care about people, whereas in my previous work experience with U.S. companies, they cared only about output and meeting the profit projections."

In this respect, the Japanese go much farther than anyone has been willing to go in America. The Japanese display what many people class as paternalism, as Abbeglen set forth in *Management and the Worker, The Japanese Solutions*.[3] The company offers its employees low-cost housing, numerous other free or low-cost services, on-site recreation facilities, and vacations at company resorts by the sea or in the mountains. Employees get increases in their incomes for marriage and for each new child. (This is true of the United Nations Organization, incidentally.) Employment is for life, up to retirement. The future of the employee and family is closely tied to the success of the company, and vice versa.

Another comprehensive report on Japanese management was written by Ezra F. Vogel of Harvard University. In 1979 he published *Japan as Number One: Lessons for America*.[4] He notes in the preface to his book that in recent years he began

3. James C. Abbeglen (New York: Harper & Row, 1973).
4. Ezra F. Vogel (Cambridge, Mass.: Harvard University Press, 1979.)

to wonder why Japan was making such signal progress in solving problems that seemed so difficult or impossible to solve in America. Always before, he said, he had never questioned the superiority of Americans in nearly all fields. Americans were well ahead, he thought—and always had thought—in their capacity for research, creativity, and practical use of natural and human resources. In the latter years of the seventies, he became preoccupied, as many Americans were, with "the decline of our confidence in government," and with the United States' seeming inability to cope with problems such as crime, unemployment, inflation, and so on.

Vogel notes that the more he studied the Japanese approach to modern organization, the business community, and the bureaucracy, the more he became satisfied that "Japanese success had less to do with [their] traditional traits than with specific organizational structures, policy programs, and conscious planning." He, as well as a number of other authors, sees many aspects of Japanese philosophy and operation that do not fit with those of the United States. But he points to a variety of successes and selective mechanisms that he believes Americans should study.

These ideas are reinforced in the report of a study published by the National Academy of Engineering in mid-1982[5] which points out that the Japanese automakers have captured so much of the United States car market because of better management, not better technology. Participative management is utilized in the successful Japanese organization, whereas American manufacturers are still using the old and less efficient authoritative-type management.

We consider next some ideas and situations that Vogel and others have pointed out, in comparison with similar ones in America.

1. The Japanese life-span is better than that of Americans

5. *The Competitive Status of the U.S. Auto Industry,* (Washington, D.C.: National Academy of Sciences, 1982).

by some four years; indeed it is the longest of any nation in the world. The figures are 72.7 years for men and 77.9 for women.

2. The infant mortality rate in Japan is the lowest in the world.

3. About 90 percent of young people complete high school in Japan. This is the highest rate in the world. The United States, at the last census, was much lower. Incidentally, Japanese students outperform all western nations in mathematics and science. In 1964, Japan in mathematics stood third in the world; the United States stood fifteenth out of nineteen countries.

4. Japanese students spend about two hundred and forty days per year in school. American students spend about one hundred and eighty days. The United States still provides students with three to four months of summer vacation. During this period they used to hoe corn and chop cotton. Today, very few do this; indeed in some areas we are hard put to find things for them to do.

5. By the time they have reached the sixth grade, most students in Japan can perform on three musical instruments. In the United States, only students in orchestras or bands are able to do this.

6. Workers in Japan are paid more than are workers in the United States.

7. The Japanese manufacture one and one-half times as much per capita as does the United States.

8. Products from Japan, which were once only cheap imitations, now dominate the world market. This is the case with respect to pianos, radios, tape-recorders, hi-fi equipment, bicycles, snowmobiles, ski equipment, zippers, cameras, and lenses, to name a few. Japanese motorcycles have eliminated the British motorcycle industry; and only Harley-Davidson is non-Japanese in America. Japanese-produced watches have now eclipsed the Swiss industry; Toyota, Datsun, and Honda dominate exports to the United States.

9. Japan produces about the same amount of steel as the United States does, but in more modern and efficient plants. In 1978, the twenty-two largest modern blast furnaces in the world included fourteen in Japan and none in the United States.

10. Japan imports more timber from the United States than it produces. And food imported by Japan from the United States requires more United States farmland to produce than is available in Japan.

11. Crime is about four times higher in the United States than it is in Japan. There are four times as many murders, five times as many rapes, and one hundred five times as many robberies in the United States as there are in Japan.

12. The standard of living in the United States used to be the first in the world.[6] This is no longer true.

13. The median pay for United States executives in large corporations is $350,000 per year. In Japan it's $104,000. This, *The Federationist* says, underscores "the American manager's proclivity for greed."[7]

Of course, not all the preceding items are directly related to Japanese management methods, but many of them are.

How did this come about? How is it that wherever Americans look in the general area of productivity, they seem to be trailing the Japanese? (Moreover, they are trailing almost ten other developed nations in terms of increase in productivity rates as has been already noted.) What are they doing that the United States is not doing? Or what is the United States doing that they are not? Whatever Americans find the differences to be, can they change the operations so that they can once again lead the world? I think they can. Whether the United States will or not depends largely on the manag-

6. Jean-Jacques Servan-Schreiber's *The World Challenge* (New York: Simon & Schuster, 1980) carries some very important information of this sort, especially in part III.

7. J. N. Ellenberger, *The Federationist, Official Magazine of the A.F.L. and C.I.O.* April–June, 1982.

ing heads of its organizations. Bottlenecks, as everyone knows, occur mainly *at the top of the bottle.*

In a general way, as I pointed out in 1974,[8] a critical review of the managerial approaches points to a much greater use in Japan of (1) the principle of participation, (2) greatly improved communications, (3) the virtual elimination of status in the organizational hierarchy, (4) far less centralization of authority, and (5) much greater concern for the employee.

Exactly how these ideas may be accurately and successfully implemented depends, of course, on the organization and those heading it. We have had numerous examples of success in one of several of the above items for the past twenty years or more. In a few signal cases, Americans have proven conclusively that certain aspects of the Japanese system work quite successfully in America. There seems little question left that great improvements in participation, communications, and concern for the employee are possible and that when they are effected, greater productivity and many side benefits result. But the elimination of status and decentralization of authority have not been achieved as well as they have in Japan, insofar as I am aware.

Pascale and Athos think that the most important aspect of Japanese organizations is that of getting everyone to try to make the company succeed, even if the company is only a little thing. The same authors note that "thousands of little people doing little things"—all with *the same basic purpose*— "can move mountains."[9]

As a further example consider the following. In a Toyota automobile factory not far from Tokyo there are, or were, eight plants arranged in cloverleaf fashion, each with two

8. William R. Van Dersal, *The Successful Manager in Government and Business* (New York: Harper & Row, 1974), pp. 186, 187. Marrow's *Failure of Success,* published in 1972, shows that a complete change in management could and did take place in about thirty months.

9. Richard T. Pascale and Anthony G. Athos, *The Art of Japanese Management, Applications for American Executives* (New York: Warner, 1981).

assembly lines. There are no human workers in this factory, only robots. In the beginning, there were some two hundred robots there; Toyota claimed that there would be seven hundred and twenty by 1982.

Production at the Toyota plant was sixty-five cars per work station per year—compared with ten to twelve for American as well as European plants. In the United States, if Americans were to move in the same direction—manufacturing entirely or almost so by robots—they would have a very considerable labor problem on their hands. Obviously, as robots replace human workers, the human workers will be thrown out of work. This situation would be intolerable.

But the impossible problem has apparently been solved in Japan. When robots replace employees, the employees are sent to one of the training schools where they learn new skills instead of heading for unemployment offices. The training course qualifies them for better-paying jobs and for more interesting new careers. These new skills usually involve microelectronics, especially that dealing with computer programming.

However, the development of software is often incredibly difficult. Excellent training courses are often required to prepare workers to do the various jobs involved. But after training, the workers can command higher salaries and far more interesting jobs. They can oftentimes get rid of the chore jobs that no one enjoys. Dr. Uenohara, director of research of Nippon Electric, is reported as saying that if they could employ the five billion inhabitants of the planet, they would still be short of personnel in Japan.

Over the long pull, Americans have produced a succession of successes. They have made many mistakes, which is likely to be true of any people intent on going somewhere. But they have scarcely hesitated; they have kept right on going. They have learned from their failures. The American record is im-

10. Servan-Schreiber, *The World Challenge*, cited earlier, pp. 182–189.

pressive and consistent, and Americans need not fear that it will be spoiled because of a couple of decades of difficulty.

At the end of the past twenty years, the United States finds itself surpassed in management by every other industrial nation in the world. It says something for America that a major part of these successes in other countries has resulted from the application of the results of American research in the sciences. American scientists have produced answers that are applicable to human beings anywhere. What the United States needs is a better understanding on the part of its managers and supervisors of the results of our own research. And then, it must urge them on to the success that is part and parcel of the American way in this world.

5

Some Techniques in Supervising

The skill with which you go about supervising comes only with practice. *How* to supervise, how to put the principles of supervision into practice, make up the art of supervision. We take up now a few ideas that may prove of value to you as a supervisor. They are not guaranteed to work with everyone, nor in every situation. But experienced and able supervisors have often found them to be of considerable value.

1. How to Begin Supervising

Assuming that you are new at the job of supervising, one way to start is to *learn all you can about your people.* This idea could well be listed as a principle of supervision, as indeed it has been in some books and pamphlets on the subject.

If you must guide and work with people, it follows at once that you must know a lot about them in order to do a good job of it. You should know about their background, their schooling, their philosophy, their habits, their attitude toward their work, their ambitions, something of their family and social life, and so on. This may seem to be a big order, and it is clear that you can never know everything about every person you supervise. But you ought to know enough to be reasonably sure what each of them is likely to do in a given set of circumstances, and how each is likely to react to your guidance. How you learn all this is up to you. A wise supervisor learns what to look for, when to ask direct questions, when to avoid questions, and when to listen. A poor supervisor is likely to judge people too quickly, to catalog them without study.

An important idea to keep in mind as you work with your people is that each person is different from every other person. We all say this to each other, but we still tend strongly to classify people into types characterized by a single factor of personality. Many of us tend to classify people by their "looks"; for example, anyone looking like the Hollywood or television version of a gangster is not to be trusted. This is unwise. People should be judged by what they do, how they think, how they act; they should not be prejudged by formula or popular misconception.

Scientifically speaking, people *are* different. As you may read in *The Human Animal* by Weston LaBarre, each of two individual parents contributes to the offspring an average of some thirty thousand genes, or inheritance factors. The number of possible sets of thirty thousand genes donated by each parent is two multiplied by itself thirty thousand times. The number of possible combinations that two parents can produce is two multiplied by itself sixty thousand times. (Two multiplied by itself only twenty-nine times will give you a figure of over a billion. Try it!) Then consider that all human beings have had a unique set of experiences that have helped to make them what they are. As LaBarre points out, all the human beings who have ever lived have simply not scratched the surface of the number of possible varieties in the human species. Recent discoveries, incidentally, indicate that the number of genes may be far greater than LaBarre's thirty thousand.

Besides this, remember that you see your people only part of the time. Their homes, their families, their hobbies, their recreation are also of great importance to them. You may see them eight hours out of twenty-four, and five days out of seven; but this is not the major portion of their lives. Your people are *whole* human beings; they are not just employees of your unit of organization.

On the basis of what you learn about each of the whole, unique human beings whose work you are to direct, you can proceed with increased confidence as you come to understand each one. All this does not mean that no two individuals will ever react the same way in a particular situation. The fact is that human beings do react similarly under certain conditions, as we will see in later chapters. Principles of supervision are based on this fact. But individuals are more likely to respond to your guidance if you treat them as individuals and not as workers or employees or subordinates.

2. How to Give Orders

An expert supervisor seldom finds it necessary to give an order to people in the form of a direct *command*. As a supervisor you have that authority, of course, and there may be times when nothing else would be effective, but these times should be rare. The best way of all—and the one requiring greatest skill—is to help your people analyze a situation in such a way that the situation itself gives the order. Both you and your people can frequently agree on the wisest course of action. This is the order, which you will be expected to state clearly as the course of action "we" should take. Orders of this kind are almost always carried out more intelligently than is an unexplained command.

These are the two extremes: direct commands versus mutual agreement on needed action. In between are a number of other ways of giving an order. They depend on the situation and on the individual. If possible, try for agreement on the best course of action. If this does not or cannot work, try suggesting. If your employee is slow to pick up suggestions, then try asking. If there is no other alternative, then you may have to use a direct command.

3. How to Get Help from Your People

There are many ways of doing a job. You can do everything of any importance yourself. Or you can pass on in advance everything any of your people want to do. In either case you may be able to get the job done. In both cases, you will probably get stomach ulcers eventually, and you may wonder why you must always replace people who are leaving your outfit. You will be, to put it mildly, a rotten supervisor.

The people under your guidance are there to do a job. As you acquire skill, you will eventually let them do it. Basing your actions on how well you know your people, you will judiciously delegate authority to make decisions and to act. You will systematically make certain that what you want done is done the way that you want it. As you work with your people to help them get the work done, you will gradually find them referring to you for help whenever they really need it, at the right time, and in the right way. As your confidence in your group grows, you will at last begin to experience the warm, fine feeling a topnotch leader gets from guiding a loyal, hard-hitting, capable bunch of people. It may even be said that you seem to have a soft job because your people seem to be doing all the work.

4. How to Make Decisions

Over and over again, your people will expect you to make decisions about the work. They will try, and they should, to influence your decisions; they will lay many facts or opinions before you; they will help you make the decisions. In the end, though, it is up to the supervisor to decide.

When a definite decision is called for, make it as promptly as possible. Be sure you know whether you have the authority to make it. You can *never* get all the facts, but be sure you have all the facts you *can* get that bear on the matter. Be sure you have weighed the facts you have and have sorted out the really important ones from the lesser ones. Then decide—and make it stick.

People will excuse a mistake now and then, but they will seldom excuse a person who never makes a clean-cut decision. Otherwise good supervisors may be lost if they dilly-dally. They will be doubly lost if they change their decisions to suit the ideas of the last person to see them. Calm, thoughtful consideration of a problem in all its facets, followed by a logical, reasoned decision, is a sure way to establishment of confidence.

5. How to Criticize

When you praise people, you should do it publicly if you possibly can. And conversely, when you must criticize or reprimand people, do it privately, *never* in the presence of a fellow worker. These are aspects of two major principles of supervision discussed in Chapter 2.

When you criticize, it is usually good business to start out by telling an employee what you like about the work. Then tell the worker what you do not like. Always tell the person why, and always do it in a friendly way, with due regard for the situation. The point is, if your employee gets the idea that you are really trying to help, that individual will be likely to take your criticism to heart. If you only make the person sore, or if the person does not understand your criticism and thinks that it is unfair, your criticism will not be worth much. Finally, be ready with a suggestion of what one can do to redeem oneself.

People usually know when they deserve criticism. If they do not get it, they may lose a certain amount of respect for their supervisor. Timeliness, therefore, is important in criticizing. Incidentally, it pays to avoid ridicule when you criticize, except under very special circumstances and when you know exactly what you are doing. All during the time you are criticizing a person for anything, keep in mind that the *dignity* of people is important to them. A person always deserves a chance to save face.[1]

6. How to Settle Grievances

Three things are important here: (a) to be careful to get all the facts you can about the grievance; (b) to get both sides, if two people or factions are involved; and (c) to settle the matter as promptly as possible. If you do not have the authority to settle things, get help from your own supervisor.

You should never ignore a grievance, no matter how trifling it may seem to you. Petty grievances have a way of growing into tough problems. Let individuals with grievances air them completely; encourage workers to talk fully about them. Sometimes the talking helps to settle them. Bear in mind that your final decision must be fair, impartial, and well understood by all concerned.

7. How to Deal with the Problem Child

Sooner or later, every supervisor gets a person in the unit who is lazy, opinionated, tactless, too slow, too fast, too talkative, moody, possessed of a persecution complex, nervous, unable to get along with other people, disloyal, discourteous, always late, never prepared, an apple-polisher—or who has some other fault that is extremely annoying or that disrupts the work generally.

Many people have the idea that the best way to deal with a problem child is to get the individual transferred somewhere else. But a personnel problem can rarely be solved this way. Where two personalities clash violently, a transfer may often be necessary; otherwise, the best place to deal with a personnel problem is right where it comes up.

1. You may find it interesting to read George Heaton, "The Dignity of the Individual," in *Readings in Management,* eds. Max D. Richards and William A. Nielander (Cincinnati: South-Western, 1958), pp. 75–81.

Each problem is different and must be met and solved on the basis of its own characteristics. Avoiding problems like these is the distinguishing mark of a poor supervisor. Attacking such problems always requires that you gain the person's confidence first. If you are reasonably sure you have it, then here is one way to proceed that is often successful:

a. As soon as you are sure of your ground, talk to the person about the fault. See if you can find out the reason for it. Be sure you explain clearly what the fault means to you, to the worker, and to the organization. Get the person to see it; then see if you can get the person to tell you how he or she expects to overcome it. Agree with the worker on a course of action, which should include your own sympathetic help whenever needed. Then tell the person, later on, how well he or she is doing.

b. If the first talk fails, try again after a reasonable interval. Go over the situation again. Search for more reasons. Try to get the person to promise to do better, and to agree on the steps he or she will take. Follow it up again; praise the person for any progress he or she makes.

c. If the fault persists and is getting serious, call the employee in again and go over the same ground once more. This takes patience, but do it with care. Then begin to consider rating, effect on opportunities, job, salary, family, and so on. Be clear about this and try to gain your employee's cooperation.

d. If there is still no progress, talk it over with your own supervisor and try to agree on a course of action. For example, the person may be warned that continuation may threaten the job—if things are that serious. He or she may be given a certain time in which to correct the fault. It may be considered with some employees that they might do better in some other type of job, possibly in another organization altogether. These more rigorous steps usually should not be taken until there is sure support "up the line."

In going forward in such a manner as this, start keeping

notes about the time you reach the third step—you can simply remember the earlier stages. You may need notes of this kind later. But do not keep a "black book," whatever you do. Again, be sure you have all the facts you can get, and go at the job in a manner that will convince problem employees that you want to help them. Always follow through, and never make threats you cannot carry out.

8. How to Deal with Misconduct

Once in a long while, a supervisor may be confronted with a suspected or clear case of misconduct or serious irregularity. These cases may range from drinking on the job, neglect of duty, or refusal to do certain kinds of work, all the way up to theft, bribery, or criminal action. What to do in such cases depends on the circumstances, of course, but there are a few things any supervisor ought to know about such matters.

In the first place, an employee action that may prove serious enough to warrant discharge, or that may land an employee in jail, is not something a supervisor can handle alone. In most government agencies and many industries, supervisors do not have the authority to fire anyone; this is reserved to the highest authorities. It is important, therefore, that you get in touch with your supervisor. The two of you must discuss the situation and decide what to do. An obvious decision might be to call in the personnel staff people of your organization for a consultation. This should not mean that you thereby wash your hands of the case. On the contrary, it is *your employee,* and you carry an important responsibility with respect to handling the case. You know, or should know, the most about the employee. You should, by all means, undertake to see the case through, insofar as your supervisory authority extends. Your recommendations should bear due weight with whatever authority makes the final decision.

In dealing with serious cases, it is of grave importance that you be sure about the facts involved. Obviously, you cannot delay indefinitely while you keep on checking. The point is that you should be in possession of sufficient information to justify whatever action you decide to take. When you intend to accuse a person of serious misconduct, you had better know where you stand. Once you are on firm ground, then act promptly.

If the situation demands immediate action, you can, in most government agencies and in some companies, (a) order the person to stop work while you get in touch with your supervisor, or (b) order the person to go with you to your supervisor, or (c) order the person to go home while you check possible next steps with your supervisor. If the person refuses to obey orders, this is classed as insubordination, and would be taken into account later when a penalty is prescribed. These statements cannot be made here with any degree of finality, because different organizations have different ideas about what authority their supervisors may exert. For this reason, you had better know what your authority is—a long time ahead of any need for action.

In terms of the many thousands of people who are at work, the number of cases of real misconduct that turn up is small. The chances are rare that you will ever have to deal with one during your entire career. Note, however, that petty matters have a habit of growing serious, and that misconduct is as preventable as are accidents.

9. How to Deal with Inefficiency

There could be many reasons for inefficiency on the part of one of your people, but there is seldom an excuse for failure on your part to deal with it promptly and effectively. Over and over again, with monotonous regularity, tough personnel problems develop in which it turns out that some employees have been getting a satisfactory performance rating although they have been inefficient all along.

Many supervisors instinctively recoil from dealing with inefficient employees on an honest basis. Telling them that they are not doing as good work as they should be can be unpleasant, if you want to make it so. If you can approach it openly and objectively, with an obvious interest in helping them, however, the task can often prove to be unexpectedly pleasant. People usually appreciate help, even though some of them may at first refuse to believe they need it. To see workers improve their work as a result of your guidance is a gratifying experience a good supervisor will cherish for a long time.

We are assuming here that you have made full use of the principles of supervision outlined in Chapter 2. Your employees know exactly what is expected of them and how much high quality work they should be turning out. You have done everything you could to keep them informed and have given them far more than ordinary help with their problems. You have pointed out their failings and worked with them to correct them. You have praised them for the things they do best. You have consulted your own supervisor and used up all the suggestions he or she could make. But in spite of considerable effort on your part, and perhaps on your supervisor's as well, over a reasonable period, they may still be unable to do their job well enough to be considered satisfactory employees. Then, *and only then,* it may be proper to try these steps:

a. Discuss the whole problem in its entirety with your own supervisor. Be objective in your appraisal of the situation and with your supervisor's help try to determine (1) whether your supervision of a particular person has been good enough, or (2) whether that person is really an unsatisfactory employee. Be honest about this. You may not have succeeded for either of these reasons. It may be that the individual deserved a trial under another supervisor. If so, proceed accordingly. If not—

b. You, and possibly your supervisor, should talk the

matter over with the person in a way that will convince him or her, if at all possible, of your fairness and genuine interest. It may be that the person should get into some other kind of work. If so, undertake to help the person find it and enlist the help of the personnel office (if the person is willing).

c. If your employee is unwilling to cooperate—and some will be—then follow through with the procedure set forth in your instructions on dealing with cases of this kind. (All supervisors should know what these instructions are; they vary with the organizations.) In doing this, be sure that you are in full possession of all pertinent facts and are fully justified in your action. Be prepared to follow through; and if dismissal or demotion is the action to take, and if the person appeals to higher authorities, which he or she has the right to do, be able to come forward with a clear, objective justification for your recommendation.

10. How to Handle Long-Distance Supervision

In many organizations, supervisors are stationed a long distance away from those whom they are expected to supervise. This makes supervision more difficult both for the workers and supervisors. Usually, the greater the distance, the more difficult it is.

I have never found an equal substitute for talking with a person face to face. On the telephone and by mail, too many ways of conveying ideas are lost that are used in personal discussion. Simple gestures, expressions, tones of voice, and the like are often as important as what is said. Nevertheless, if your people are at a distance, there are various expedients available; and all of them depend for their success largely on how systematically they are used. Some of these are:

a. *Work plans.* The only satisfactory way for you to know what your people intend to do is to get from them a written plan. The plan can be simple, and it can be made for a period no longer than between your visits—or it can be made on a monthly, quarterly, or yearly basis. The plans should be changed as often as necessary, but they are a very important source of information for you. By using them you can give guidance when needed. For long-distance work they are almost mandatory.

Note that the plans must be your people's, not yours. *They* should make them and follow them. If you formalize them too much and require too many things to be in them they may easily become a burden. Plans are only statements of intention and should be used accordingly.

b. *Meetings.* You will need to hold meetings of your people at regular intervals—with due regard for travel costs, travel time, and interruption of regular work. These meetings will demand thoughtful and careful planning on your part and on the part of your people, so that the time you have is used in the most profitable way. Your people ought to know when they are to be held a long time ahead, so that they can plan their work.

These meetings make possible a review of recent work and discussions of plans for the next period. Here also can be arranged the special training you may want your people to have. In meetings, you have one of two possibilities for working face to face with your people. Use these meetings as valuable tools, never as unplanned, semisocial get-togethers. (Develop the social angle in the evenings.)

c. *Regular visits.* As often as the load of work permits, and as regularly as possible, you will need to visit each of your people at their work location. Your people should know, well in advance, when you are coming. They can then present their problems at one time and plan their own activities sensibly. When you get there, stay long enough to do an adequate job. Encourage your people to prepare for your visit and to be clear about the kind of help they want. Plan also what you want to get done.

The practice of dropping in unexpectedly, upheld by many people, is unsound. It not only makes it impossible to use time to best advantage, but it tends to build distrust and even fear, not confidence. *Always* write or phone when you cannot be there at your regular time. This is only ordinary courtesy expected from anyone.

d. *Reports.* If your meetings and visits are sufficient to maintain good communications, you may not need to ask for reports. Certainly you will do well to avoid them if you can. If they prove to be necessary, then by all means keep them as simple as possible. A weekly letter may often serve admirably, provided your employees know pretty well what information you want. If your people are required to make reports by other offices of your organization, by all means use these yourself to avoid having your people do double work.

e. *Other devices.* Long-distance supervision almost forces the development of manuals or handbooks of some sort, in which procedures, policies, standards, methods, or other matters are clearly set forth. Sometimes these are overdone, but they are valuable if they are used with common sense.

PERFORMANCE REVIEW
Merlyn C. Meyen[2]

Supervisors all have one thing in common. They are supposed to be leaders. Leadership is the ability of a supervisor

2. Meyen is in charge of the Extension Service program in Cook County, Illinois, the location of Chicago. He has a staff of twenty-one professional workers plus a number of administrative and secretarial workers; his annual budget is close to $2 million. He wrote this material in early 1980 and submitted it as a paper in a three-week class in supervision at the Extension Winter School, University of Arizona.

I felt that this simple description of performance review and appraisal was the best I had seen; I requested permission to use it in this book. Mr. Meyen gave me his permission, providing that I noted that as references he used "Guides For Supervisors" Series 1 through 18, University of Illinois; and Extension Service, U.S. Department of Agriculture's "Supervising Paraprofessionals."

to accomplish through others the work or goals of a particular unit. When this is done successfully, both the employee and the supervisor will experience great personal satisfaction.

The supervisor is responsible for giving answers to basic questions certain to be uppermost in the minds of responsible staff members. The questions would be:

What am I expected to do?
How well am I expected to do it?
How well am I doing it?
How can I do it better?
How can I qualify for a more responsible position?

Employee performance reviews should be an indispensable part of a supervisor's role to help ensure that goals are achieved or exceeded. Staff morale, productivity, job satisfaction, working relations, and career advancement depend upon clear answers to the basic questions.

Frequency and Timing of Performance Reviews

Reviewing employee performance is an all-the-time responsibility. There is no substitute for a continuing person-to-person communication between employees and supervisor throughout the year. Planned and scheduled performance appraisals are desirable in addition to the ongoing or continuing evaluations.

Performance reviews should be conducted after about six months of on-the-job experience. In addition, all professional staff should participate in a performance appraisal during the months of February, March, or April. This allows the process to be completed before the time salary recommendations are made for the next contract year. The formal appraisal will serve as the culminating phase of a continuing process.

Conducting the Performance Appraisal

The performance review need not follow a rigid format and need not be tightly structured. Printed forms are probably desirable in appraisals with professional staff, but the main thing is to have an effective performance review.

A skillful supervisor leads employees to evaluate themselves. Performance should be emphasized, not personality. Attempt problem solving and developing insight; be professional about this.

Before the session begins have objectives of the meeting clearly in mind and have required background information at hand.

During the session make it a two-way discussion; listen as well as talk. Highlight the positive as much as possible and show interest in what the staff member has to say. Encourage the staff members to talk about situations and problems. Take the attitude that you can learn as well as teach.

Before the session ends, show and tell that you appreciate the good features of the staff member's work performance. Help the employee relate personal goals to future performance. Ask "Is there anything else you would like to discuss?"

When the session ends, be sure that the staff member has a clear understanding of what must be done. Always leave the door open for further discussion.

Performance Standards

The first question that must be answered in a performance review is: What quality and quantity of work have been produced? The answer to the question by itself may not necessarily reflect the staff member's performance. A staff member's work output can be favorably or unfavorably affected by factors other than his or her own individual performance.

The work environment may not be conducive to high productivity and quality. A 4-H youth program being introduced to a predominately minority neighborhood may take much longer to enroll good members and achieve high-quality programs as compared with the same program being introduced into a predominately white middle-class community.

Do not compare the staff member's work output with that of another specific individual, especially that of a coworker. Make it clear that the staff member's performance is being judged against established standards which reflect how others have performed under similar circumstances.

At the conclusion of the appraisal, the supervisor and staff member should have a common understanding of what work the staff member has performed and how well it has been done. They should identify steps to be taken to correct any unsatisfactory situation. If additional training could improve the staff member's performance, the supervisor should guide the staff member to receive the needed training.

Overall Appraisal

In addition to performance appraisal, the review process should also include an overall appraisal. This will serve as a guide to assess what can be expected of a staff member in the future. Annual appraisal will reflect how effective a supervisor is in supervising and developing an employee.

A work performance appraisal considers a short period of time, and no attempt at a final "score" or "rating" is made. An annual overall appraisal is really a performance appraisal considering a specific and longer period of time. A score or rating is established based on the staff member's performance.

A simple example would be evaluating the following points:

Amount of work.

Quality of work.

Timeliness and dependability.

Initiative.

Ability to assume responsibility.

Ability to work as team member.

The supervisor must evaluate or pass judgment about the staff member's performance in relation to these factors. Overall performance might be evaluated in the following terms:

1. *Outstanding.* Performance consistently exceeds the standard by a wide margin. Occasionally a contribution is made that is of significant value. Exceptionally good performance is the rule and is more than occasional.

2. *Superior.* Performance exceeds requirements fairly consistently. Occasional instances of outstanding work. Below-standard performance seldom occurs. Only very limited supervision is required.

3. *Satisfactory.* Relatively few instances when performance is substandard. Occasional instance of superior performance. Normal supervision is required.

4. *Below average.* Generally meets the minimum performance standards. Close supervision and review of work is necessary. Needs improvement.

5. *Unsatisfactory.* Poor performance occurs too frequently and is of such a nature that the work of the organization may be adversely affected. Work performance below minimum standard for continued employment.

Staff Member's Development

Consider whether previously agreed upon training has had a positive effect on the staff member's performance. While past performance is being appraised, the real focus will be on the staff member's future performance and development. The supervisor should enter judgments concerning the progress made by the staff member, activities that the staff member can utilize to develop further, and supportive action that the supervisor can take. The staff member should be given the opportunity to establish several goals for the coming year. The goals should also be recorded and become part of the basis for future performance appraisals. (*Note:* The above paragraph explains the exact process that resulted in my attending the 1980 Extension Winter School.)

Conclusion

The best way to evaluate a performance appraisal is to ask the question: Did it accomplish what it was intended to do? The purpose of a performance appraisal is:

1. To ensure that the staff member
   a. Understands what is expected of him or her.
   b. Is told how well he or she is doing.
   c. Is told how to improve his or her performance.
   d. Is informed how he or she can continue to progress to greater earnings.

2. To provide a communication tool to help the supervisor
   a. Get the optimum contribution from the staff member.
   b. Develop the staff member.
   c. Maintain an accurate assessment of the capabilities of the staff member.
   d. Maintain good employee morale.
   e. Eliminate potential disciplinary problems.

3. To keep higher administration informed about
   a. The present capabilities and future potential of the staff.

b. The availability of qualified employees to fill future staffing needs.

Performance appraisal requires care and skill. Poor handling may result in appraisals that are unjust. One of the first challenges to a person in a major supervising role will be to master the fundamental skills of performance review.

6

Participation

In April 1927 an experiment with human beings got under way at the Hawthorne Plant of the Western Electric Company at Chicago. This experiment, plus some others, and their surprising results have had a profound influence on the whole field of management and supervision for many years. They have been called a breakthrough in management.

The stated objective of this experiment was to find answers to such questions as these:

1. Do employees actually get tired out?
2. Are rest pauses desirable?
3. Is a shorter working day desirable?
4. Why does production fall off in the afternoon?
5. How do employees feel about the company?
6. What effects would changes in working equipment have?

To make the study, six experienced "female operators" were chosen to be the guinea pigs. Two of the women, who were friends, were asked to select four other women. These women worked at the job of putting together a telephone relay. Each relay took about a minute to put together. All day long, day after day, the women assembled about thirty-five small parts and secured them in position with four machine screws. This was monotonous, repetitive work, and it is not surprising that the researchers wondered whether fatigue played a part in production.

The experiment began simply enough. The women were invited to the superintendent's office, and the test was explained to them. They were willing to take part in it, but the record notes that they were shy at the first conference. During the first two weeks, then, a record was kept of the production of each woman, that is, of the number of relays she put together per hour, per day, and per week. The average was about 2,400 per week. The researchers kept the record by means of an ingenious electric counting device that punched a hole in a traveling paper tape every time a woman put a finished relay in the chute alongside her bench. Also, in this two-week period, the women were given complete physical examinations. According to the physician's report, they were "six normally functioning organisms."

Two weeks after the study began, the women were moved into a special experimental room, which was simply a corner of the regular shop room, closed off by partitions. Temperature and humidity readings were made every hour, and a test observer made notes of remarks made by the women and of anything else that the observer thought was significant. And for five weeks nothing else was done. The women went on assembling parts, and the electric recorder mechanically noted how many they finished. The idea was to get the women used to the new conditions.

After five weeks the experimenters made a change. Each woman had formerly been paid so much per relay, based on the average piece rate for about a hundred workers in the big shop. The change was to a new rate based on that of her own little group in the experimental room. This meant that each woman could earn an amount more nearly in proportion to her own individual efforts. Nothing else was changed for two months. During this time the women produced relays a little faster than they had before. In the records maintained by the company, this was called Period Three. During Period Three, output was up slightly.

At this time the more significant experimental work was begun—or so the researchers believed. They gave the women two rest pauses of five minutes each, one at ten in the morning, one at two in the afternoon. These breaks were discussed with the women—this was a regular practice all during the tests—and they thought five-minute pauses would be better than ones of ten or fifteen minutes. If the pauses were too long, they felt, it might be hard to make up the lost time. This change seems simple now that the coffee break is such a common custom in America, but at the time, it was unusual. This was Period Four, lasting for five weeks. Production definitely went up.

In the next period, the pauses were lengthened to ten minutes each. The change lasted a month, and during that time the daily and weekly output went up—higher than it ever had before.

Next, in Period Six, the women got six rest periods a day for five minutes each. The researchers kept this up for a month, but the women did not like the constant interruption, and their output fell off slightly.

In Period Seven, the pauses were changed to a fifteen-minute morning break and a ten-minute afternoon break. In addition, the company provided refreshments. Production went up again and stayed up for the eleven weeks of this period.

Following this, the experimenters continued these same pauses but changed some other conditions. They stopped work half an hour earlier each day. Production went up. Then they stopped work a full hour earlier each day. Rates of production went up, although the total fell off slightly. Later, the work week was cut from five and a half days to five days. The daily output was increased, but the weekly output was slightly down.

The researchers began to wonder what was happening. It

seemed to them (as it may have to you) that no matter what they did, the women continued to produce more and more and more. They began to wonder. Then they decided, with the full concurrence of the women, on a bold and conclusive stroke. They would return to the beginning—no rest periods, no refreshments, no shortened hours. Obviously, production should fall to what it was in the beginning. This was supposed to be a scientific experiment; all the conditions were apparently clear and controlled; production, therefore, should be related to the experimental conditions introduced.

It is to the credit of Western Electric researchers that they decided on this return to original conditions. After all, some of their questions had been answered: rest pauses were obviously desirable; so were shorter working days. But at any rate, in September 1928, eighteen months after the tests had begun, everything was changed back to what it had been in the beginning. The researchers felt that production should have dropped also, back to about what it was to start with.

Instead, *production rose to a point higher than it had ever been before,* and stayed that way for three months.

With a certain doggedness the experimenters pushed ahead. In the next period they went back to the fifteen-minute break in the morning and the ten-minute break in the afternoon. But this time the women had to provide their own refreshments. Production climbed to even greater heights. During this period the women were assembling three thousand relays a week—25 percent more than they had been producing to start with, and the output was steady and continuous.

One gains the impression that the researchers were considerably puzzled over the continual increase in production. Their reports spoke of the "astonishing" upward trend in output, regardless of the kinds of changes introduced. Improvements in output were to be expected as a result of the rest pauses; after all, the work *was* monotonous, and breaks should have helped relieve the monotony. But how explain that the return to monotony, which should have resulted in a decrease in output, instead resulted in a new high in production?

The answer to the question turned out to have nothing much to do with the rest pauses, or the shortened hours, or refreshments. It had to do instead with a change in mental attitude of the female operators. This came about as a result of two or possibly three major changes that were overlooked in the beginning. The first of these was that the experimental room was put in charge of an interested and sympathetic chief observer who replaced the gang boss the women were used to. The chief observer was interested in each woman and her output; and furthermore, his attitude convinced the women of his interest and pride in their achievements. The clincher for this point lies in a remark made by one of the women: "I hope I never see a gang boss again," said she. "We don't have to worry about getting bawled out about our rates up here."

The change from gang boss to chief observer meant a complete change in supervision. This was a major difference in itself. But there is more to it than that. The new supervisor—the observer—was *not* under the direction of the regular plant organization, as the gang boss had been. He was directed by the research group, to whom he was responsible. Moreover, the group of six women was physically cut off from the rest of the company organization by the walls of the experimental room. All this was, in fact, an organizational change of great significance, although it has not been generally recognized as such. In recent years, from other research, we have learned that a simple change in supervisors—whether through training of the person or replacement by another—will not necessarily effect any great change in the group supervised. What must also occur is the right kind of a change in the organization above that will give the person the freedom to operate in an enlightened way. If both supervisory and organizational changes are made in such a way as to complement each other, then changes in production, morale, and so on can be effected.

The third important change that had been introduced was that the various experimental changes were discussed in advance with the women. At first, they were shy and uneasy, suspicious of the executives whom they were meeting. Later on, they gained confidence and spoke out frankly, as they found their ideas listened to and used. For the first time in their working lives these women were being treated as human beings instead of female operators. And also for the first time, they were *participating* in the planning of their own work. It seemed that when you treat people as human beings, they respond as human beings. And when they play a part in planning their own work, they outdo themselves in executing it.

These three changes in supervision, organization, and participation supplement and complement each other. Each must take place if the others are to be effective. Possibly this illustrates the need for coordination—that is, for a working together—of many factors, if the management is to be the best we can achieve. Here, however, we must look a little further into the idea of participation and to consider how we can make use of it.

The experiments at the Hawthorne Plant went on for five years. The conditions of Period Seven, with the fifteen-minute break in the morning and the ten-minute break in the afternoon, were carried on as standard for the group. High output was maintained all this time, so that any excitement over the tests was clearly lost. The researchers felt, as the years passed, that something permanent had been achieved. And so it had.

Participation at the Lincoln Electric Company

In 1895 the Lincoln Electric Company went into business making and repairing electric motors in John Lincoln's basement in Cleveland. Twelve years later James Lincoln, John's younger brother, joined the company. In 1914 James became the general manager of the business, which was still small and in poor shape financially.

One of the first things James Lincoln did was to get all the people in the company together. He asked them to elect representatives from each department to an advisory board. This group was to provide him with advice and counsel on how best to run the company. Lincoln had the idea that if he could get all the employees to want the company to succeed as badly as he did, there ought to be no limits to what they could do together. This board was purely advisory. Lincoln ran the company, but he listened to the board's ideas and suggestions. Since that time, the advisory board has met twice every month, through and including 1983.

This innovation was made at the beginning of the First World War. During that war, Lincoln Electric developed arc welding, not only for repair purposes but for factory production of machinery and equipment. Later, in World War II, arc welding made possible the production of the Liberty ship fleet. Lincoln has specialized in this field ever since and has now become the largest manufacturer of arc-welding equipment in the world.

But to get back to the development of the business:

In 1915 the company gave each employee a paid-up life insurance policy.

In 1919 the employees formed an association to provide for health benefits and social activities.

By 1923 every employee was getting a two-week paid vacation.

In 1925 the employees were able to buy stock in the company.

In 1929 the board of directors set up a suggestion system.

In 1934 the company began distributing bonuses to employees from profits remaining after taxes and relatively conservative dividends. Each employee received a check, the size of which depended on the quality of his or her performance during the year. According to a Lincoln Electric financial statement, the total bonuses paid out have very nearly equaled the total annual compensation payments from 1934 to the present time. More recent examples are: year-end bonus in 1979, $44 million; in 1980, $43 million; in 1981, $55 million.

During the ten years following 1934, a whole series of other ideas was set in motion. A pension plan was set up, paid for by the company; by 1964 the company had purchased retirement annuities for all employees at a cost of $13 million. A policy of guaranteed employment was established and followed. A merit rating plan was developed for deciding on each person's share of the bonus. Promotion from within was established as a policy. A job evaluation procedure was set up to determine rates of base pay. All the foregoing ideas have been carried on since their inception. Many of them came from suggestions made by the advisory board.

During the period of thirty years from 1934 to 1964, the Lincoln Electric Company experienced some great increases in their costs of manufacturing. For the principal materials used in the making of arc-welding equipment, the cost of steel increased 300 percent; the cost of copper went up 377 percent. Moreover, the cost of labor rose to a figure that was 547 percent above its cost in 1934.

In view of these increasing costs, it is natural to expect that the price of the arc-welding equipment must have gone up in proportion—up, say, to 300 or 400 percent of the 1934 prices. Instead, the company has been able to *reduce the cost of its product by 20 percent.*

A final indication of the success of Lincoln Electric policies may be seen in the monthly rate of separation, or turnover rate, of the employees. Since 1945 the turnover in all industry has been eight to ten times that of the turnover at Lincoln Electric. The rate in 1959 for all industry was 3.3

percent; for Lincoln it was 0.33 percent. This figure was correct as late as 1983. This means that on the average, industry was losing better than three workers out of a hundred each month, whereas it took nine months for Lincoln Electric to lose three workers.

A number of factors have been at work in this situation:

1. All the employees have participated in the running of the company through their representatives of the advisory board and through their active suggestion system.

2. All the employees have profited from both their ideas and suggestions and the efficiency of their work. The profits have taken concrete form in bonuses, life insurance, pensions, paid vacations, health benefits, and the dividends from stock purchases.

3. No employee has had to fear a layoff; job security has depended on each employee's own efforts, not on factors over which he or she had no control.

4. Promotion has depended on a person's efforts. He or she could count on competition with associates rather than with people with influence brought into the company from outside.

James Lincoln believed that the full-fledged participation or cooperation of the entire working staff of the company accounts for its remarkable successes. He noted:

> Cooperation is the working together of all people in the organization. . . . It means the enthusiastic *finding* of new methods, new tools, new ideas, by all people, from top to bottom in the organization. . . . Cooperation means the enthusiastic *use* by all people in the company of their best ideas, skills, and methods to reduce costs and improve quality.[1]

Lincoln believed that the money incentive (i.e., bonuses) alone does very little to gain the cooperation of workers.

1. James F. Lincoln, *A New Approach to Industrial Economics* (New York: Devin-Adair, 1961). A readable and interesting work, despite its somewhat ponderous title.

Workers must be sure that their greater efficiency will indeed bring them greater rewards both in cash and in other ways. This, of course, has been a fact at Lincoln Electric.

Some Additional Ideas about Participation

A supervisor who has thought critically about the job of supervision comes eventually to realize that what a group of people can accomplish depends upon the degree to which each member of the group is genuinely interested in the work. This interest may have developed initially for all sorts of reasons, but it increases substantially in proportion to the opportunity people have to take part in planning their own work and in deciding how to do it.

Douglas McGregor, professor of management at the Massachusetts Institute of Technology, put it this way:

> One theme . . . recurs with remarkable frequency in reports of social science research on human relations, and of the experimentation of the management pioneers. Its significance . . . depends upon whether it is imbedded in a philosophy of management or regarded as merely another fancy technique.
>
> This recurrent theme is that of "participation." You will find it—with wide or limited emphasis—in McCormick's "multiple management," in Carey's "consultative supervision," in Given's "bottom-up management," in Barnard's "executive authority," and in a score of other well-known principles enunciated by management pioneers.
>
> You will see its implications and its applications in much recent research—for example in the work of the late Kurt Lewin and his associates in the Research Center for Group Dynamics, and in the work of Rensis Likert and his Survey Research Center, of E. Wight Bakke, of Burleigh Gardiner, or Joseph Scanlon, of Alexander Leighton, of Robert Merton, of Alex Bavelas, and dozens of other social scientists and consultants in many different companies and universities. Surely an idea which is so often reiterated must have more than casual significance.

So much for the background of research. Now for what participation can do, McGregor goes on to say:

> It provides opportunities to bring into the work situation a variety of "on-the-job" satisfactions. It offers a potential path through the maze of problems connected with technical efficiency in plant layout, process, and work methods. It gives recognition to people as human beings, individually and in their group relations, and it brings dignity and meaning to their jobs. It can tap the creative imagination and inventive ingenuity for which we Americans are justly famous. It can banish fear and dependence by giving the members of the organization an opportunity to exert control over their own destinies and to acquire genuine understanding of what are usually felt to be mysterious and arbitrary management actions. It offers, *par excellence,* a way to encourage the development of genuine personal responsibility among all members of the organization, and with it the freedom which is always lacking when control is centralized.... It is, incidentally, the principle which underlies our democratic society.[2]

Ideas of this kind lead to the conclusion that a supervisor is not there just to "whip up the horses," so to speak, and make them work as hard as they can. Rather, the supervisor's job is to get the willing, zestful cooperation of the people in accomplishing a job which they have had a hand in planning, and which they want to do because they see it as *their* work, *their* opportunity, and *their* responsibility. The will to do must come from *within* the people, not from outside.

How then can you as a supervisor get this willing, cooperative, zestful effort from people? You get it by such means as these:

1. Keep your people fully and currently informed of everything you learn that in any way affects the work they are doing or plan to do. This is an echo of our second princi-

2. Douglas M. McGregor, "Changing Patterns in Human Relations," *Management Record,* September 1950, pp. 322–323 and 366–368.

ple of supervision—that people must have guidance in doing their work. The supervisor, being designated by grade, salary, title, and authority as a leader of the group, is in a position to know first, ahead of anyone else, what the organization plans to do, what changes may be contemplated, and what effect any such changes may have on the unit. It is to the supervisor that orders come, written or oral, to take actions. In order to keep your people with you, it behooves you to see that information of this kind is passed on to your people promptly.

2. Seek the advice and counsel of all the people in the development of decisions that will affect the work they are doing. In seeking this counsel, you are bound to consider it seriously and sincerely. It may well be that you cannot take their recommendations in every instance. When you cannot, or when you can take them only in part, you must explain clearly why you cannot. Your people will usually recognize that since you are held responsible for the results of the decisions, it is you who must make them. They will respect your decisions when they understand, even though they may not necessarily agree with them. It is easier for people to do this *if* they have had their full say, and *if* they understand why. Otherwise, following a leader is pretty much a matter of blind loyalty.

3. Work with your people in attempting to solve problems facing the unit. If your people come to see these problems as *their* problems and, furthermore, if they have an active part in solving them, then the solutions are also *theirs*. It may often happen that you know, or believe you know, exactly what the solution ought to be. Nevertheless, it is wiser for you first to explain the problem clearly, then participate with your people in its solution. Repeatedly, experienced supervisors will tell you (no less than the social scientists) that while there are often many possible solutions, the one that the group of people can agree on is the one most likely to

succeed. This, of course, is because it is the people who must try to make the solution work.

There is a pitfall to be avoided here. Supervisors who regularly try to get their people merely to approve their own solution are in for trouble. This is not participation; it is manipulation; and few people enjoy the feeling of having been used.

4. Share with your people the setting of goals or objectives and the performance standards for reaching them. The establishment of objectives is most commonly a job for the whole group. The setting of performance standards is necessarily individual in character, although shared by the supervisor and each person. Even here, however, the group as a whole may contribute, since how each individual may perform is related to how other individuals should perform also.

We can summarize these four points in a single idea: full participation of people in the planning and conduct of their work makes it possible for them to apply their whole intelligence to the task. This is a different thing from doing only what someone else, i.e., their supervisor, tells them to do. The idea is well summarized by E. Wight Bakke, former director of the Yale University Labor and Management Center, who notes that

> It is no bed of roses and certainly no panacea for human relations problems between management and the managed. There are testimonies from managerial experience as to both successes and failures. But much evidence from psychological and social science research as well as from many outstanding practical experiments indicates that such a practice is based on a sound principle derived from the nature of human beings and their management in the doing of productive work.
>
> The principle I have in mind is that self-realization in our culture is intimately bound up with the degree to which people are able to participate, under intelligent and rational leader-

ship, and the degree to which they have an effective voice, in determining the rules and conditions under which, and the plans according to which, they live and work.[3]

This is a long sentence to be sure, but it is worth reading many times.

At this point, the reader will do well to turn to page 108 and to review the material headed "System 4." This is a brief description of what participation can mean in an organization, as studied at the University of Michigan by Rensis Likert.

Some Problems in Participation

There are a number of reasons that can be and have been advanced to show why participation will not or cannot work. These we must review because, as Bakke says, there have indeed been both successes and failures with the idea. Here are some of them:

1. If we let the workers have as much to say as is implied in the idea of participation, we will have anarchy. And this we would have of course, *if* (a) there were no agreement, to start with, on what the organization was established to do, and (b) if there were no "intelligent and rational leadership" exerted. But given these two conditions, the principle of participation has been wonderfully successful in too many situations to warrant discarding it. Anarchy does not result; instead, productivity frequently booms, just as it did with the women at Western Electric.

2. Setting goals, planning, coordinating, decision making, and controlling are functions that can only be correctly and properly exercised by top management, that is, by the supervisors occupying the higher positions in the organization.

Let us consider, however, who it is that finally makes deci-

3. E. Wight Bakke, "The Function of Management," in *Human Relations and Modern Management,* ed. E. M. Hugh-Jones (Amsterdam, Holland: North-Holland, 1958), pp 241–242.

sions effective, carries out plans, and coordinates efforts. Is it the "big boss"? Is it the supervisor of a unit? Or is it the people who are doing the work? The boss may "plan" on turning out certain work by a January 1 deadline; but the people turn out the work, and it is they who meet the deadline, *if it is met.* Executives may think that they are "coordinating," but if they are successful, it is because the people are willing to work together. Any executive of experience can tell you that plans have a habit of going wrong when the people who must carry them out simply do not have their hearts in the job.

3. If we let the workers participate in planning, making important decisions, and the like, the supervisor will lose prestige and authority will deteriorate. But the reverse has proved true in actual practice. People have respect for and enjoy working with a leader who seeks their advice and who gives it careful consideration. They can and do respect a person who works effectively *with* them. And when a person gains the respect of the people, how can it be said that he or she has lost prestige? The fact is, as John Cowper Powys noted long ago in his *Meaning of Culture,* that in throwing away one's soul, one frequently saves it. And with respect to authority it may be questioned whether the conventional authority is really necessary. A skillful supervisor is able to get people to establish a goal and work hard to reach it. He or she need not *command* them, but only make it possible for them to exert their intelligence to set and reach such a goal.

4. Participation is another one of those management fads that will have its day in the sun and then disappear into the limbo of forgotten notions. But the idea has been too widely and successfully practiced; it has persisted too long; and it has repeatedly been reinforced by research in many fields, often unexpectedly. It is an idea on which our system of government is based, and there has not yet appeared anywhere in the world a better idea. It is an idea firmly fixed in many of the world's greatest religions, so it may therefore be said to

have important ethical roots. Far from being a fad, the idea of participation may, as McGregor says, "offer a potential path" through a maze of problems in the field of management.

It would be well for any supervisor to accord careful study to the meaning and uses of the participation idea. It is possible to experiment with it; for example, in Chapter 11 there is a discussion of methods to use in improving operating efficiency. The most fruitful of these relies heavily on participation. It has been successfully used in industrial, business, and government organizations even without the supervisory and organizational changes that ought to accompany it for fullest effectiveness. A radical change from existing supervisory practice may not be necessary; step-by-step change is apparently possible. Even so, complete changeover to participative operation is likely to produce even greater results.

One last word of caution is necessary. This is aimed especially at organizations in which participation is little used, if at all, and in which the only thing the workers have to do is what they are told. The caution is this: Supervisors using participation as a regular basis for their supervisory practice feel that it requires more skill and intelligence than supervisory practice based on the old boss-subordinate idea. Experienced supervisors who have tried to change have told me that it was harder work than what they had been doing under their old system. Many of them added, however, that it was not only more effective, once they got it going, but that after a while ("when you get used to it") it became easy.

As Robert K. Burns pointed out in the April 1959 issue of *Public Personnel Review*, "the art of leadership, in the words of a great general, consists in getting people to do what you want done because they want to do it."

7

Something about Motivation

In 1959 Frederick Herzberg and his associates in Pittsburgh published a report on their research entitled *The Motivation to Work.*[1] These psychologists had been trying to get a convincing answer to the question: What do people want from their jobs? They wanted to find out what factors affect workers' attitudes or feelings toward their jobs. They also wanted to know whether these feelings made any difference in the way people work, that is, in how productive they are.

Of course, many other scientists had worked on this problem, and the Pittsburgh investigators reviewed everything they could find that had been done before.[2] In general, they were not satisfied that the published information could answer these questions conclusively. But in reviewing the literature they did find one possibly important idea. They noticed that when the investigators asked people what they *liked* about their jobs, they got one kind of answer; when they asked people what they *did not like* about their jobs, they got

1. Frederick Herzberg, Bernard Mausner, and B. B. Snyderman, *The Motivation to Work* (New York: Wiley, 1959).
2. The results of this review work were also published: Frederick Herzberg, et al., *Job Attitudes: Review of Research and Opinion* (Psychological Services of Pittsburgh, 1957).

another kind of answer. It seemed from this that there might be a difference between the factors that had to do with good feelings about a job and the factors that had to do with bad feelings.

So the Pittsburgh investigators started to study people's attitudes about their jobs with such an idea in mind. They made their study in nine companies in and around Pittsburgh, and they aimed it at engineers and accountants, a hundred of each. They used a very simple approach. "Think of a time," they asked each person, "when you felt exceptionally good about your job—either the one you have now or any other job you have had. Tell us what happened." They checked each person's story very carefully. When did this happen? How long did you feel good? Why did this make you feel good? How long did you feel this way? How did this affect the way you did your job? These and many more questions were aimed at getting as clear and specific answers as possible. As soon as one story was completed, the investigators asked for another, this time one of when a person felt very bad about something that happened on the job. And again, a series of questions seeking clear and specific answers.

All told, the investigators obtained about 476 such stories from the 200 engineers and accountants. Next they analyzed critically what they had found. This is a well-known technique—the interview and then analysis of the answers—that is regularly used by psychologists and by analysts of public opinion polls. In their report, the investigators recorded exactly how they analyzed the information, how they coded it, how they checked the accuracy of their coding, and so on. This account is of great interest to other scientists, but we can simply note here that the job was well and carefully done. The results are what may be of greatest interest to supervisors.

The Job-Satisfying Factors

The investigators found five factors or ideas that the people mentioned most often when they talked about feeling good about their jobs. Arranged in the order of frequency with which they were mentioned, these were:

1. Achievement.
2. Recognition.
3. The work itself.
4. Responsibility.
5. Advancement.

This is what the investigators meant by these factors:

1. *Achievement.* This factor was mentioned most often. In the stories about good feelings, some 41 percent revolved around something the people had done that was successful. There were all kinds of stories about many kinds of jobs. In each one, though, the workers felt that they had done something in which they could take pride. They were satisfied and pleased with their achievement.

2. *Recognition.* Here the people told how someone recognized their good work and complimented them in some way about it. They got a pat on the back from a customer, or the boss, or an associate, or a subordinate. Usually the recognition was associated with achievement.

3. *The work itself.* This factor involved work that was interesting, challenging, or varied or that could be carried through from beginning to end. The engineers and accountants got great satisfaction out of working at creative tasks, whether recognition came or not.

4. *Responsibility.* Under this factor, people talked about jobs they did without supervision, for which they were fully responsible. Sometimes this was responsibility for a new kind of work, without advancement; sometimes it was responsibility for the work of other people.

5. *Advancement.* This means that the employee was promoted. In half the stories, the promotion was a surprise; the person had not expected it. This factor usually involved increases in pay, but in the study it was separated from salary, as a factor in itself.

Good feelings that came to the people for these five reasons tended to last a long time after the events involved. Interestingly, the good feelings about responsibility, the work itself, and advancement lasted longest of all. This trio is much more potent, so to speak, than is achievement or recognition insofar as their lasting effects are concerned. On the other hand, achievement and recognition head the list of factors that are most frequently associated with people's satisfaction about their jobs. In any event, it turned out that these factors were closely associated with each other, and that they were responsible in largest part for feelings of satisfaction that the workers had about their jobs.

The Job-Dissatisfying Factors

Next the Pittsburgh investigators turned to the factors that were mentioned most often by the people as they told about instances when they were unhappy about their jobs. As the investigators had expected, the factors leading to job dissatisfaction were not the same as the factors just discussed. Instead, different factors appeared in most of the accounts. These were:

1. Company policy and administration.
2. Technical supervision.
3. Salary.
4. Interpersonal supervision.
5. Working conditions.

Again, we list these and explain what the investigators meant by them:

1. *Company policy and administration.* This had to do with

company inefficiency, waste, duplication of effort, or a struggle for power. But more of the stories that mentioned this factor had to do with personnel and other policies that were unfair or positively harmful to the people. Frequently, salary was mentioned along with policy and administration.

2. *Technical supervision.* This factor had nothing to do with social relations between the employees and their supervisors (see factor 4, below, for this) but with lack of competence on the part of the supervisor. Supervisors were mentioned who simply did not know how to supervise the technical work for which they were responsible, or who were unfair.

3. *Salary.* This factor was mentioned in both the good stories and the bad. However, in the stories of unhappy feelings, salary was mentioned as part of an unfair system of wage administration. In the stories of good feelings, salary was simply part of advancement, hence good. The scientists concluded that unfair handling of salaries—wage increases given too late or reluctantly, or too little difference between the salaries of new and older employees—was, therefore, a factor of most importance in leading to dissatisfaction.

4. *Interpersonal supervision.* This factor refers to the personal relations between the workers and their supervisor. When the employees could not get along with their boss, they felt bad about their jobs. Frequently this factor was closely associated with factor 2, poor technical supervision.

5. *Working conditions.* This had to do with poor facilities, inconvenient location of the plant, and the amount of work the employees had to do on the job. It is to the credit of those interviewed that they complained of not enough work rather than too much.

The workers' unhappy feelings about their jobs came largely as a result of the operation of these five factors. There were two additional feelings the workers mentioned very frequently as a result. They felt that the company was unfair. And they felt that they were not getting anywhere in their jobs. The stories they told, in which they mentioned one or more of the five factors, were of events that made them feel that they were being treated unfairly and that prospects for professional growth looked pretty grim.

Parenthetically, we may note here that expert supervision can throw the five satisfying factors into full operation—at least as supervision is defined and used in this book. In the study we are discussing here, supervision, both technical and interpersonal, has a special meaning given to it by the investigators. It would be well not to confuse the two meanings.

Some Conclusions about the Factors

The findings talked about so far lead to the following general conclusions:

1. There are five factors of importance that lead people to be satisfied and happy with their jobs. These are achievement, recognition, the challenge of the work itself, responsibility, and advancement. These factors revolve around the idea that people want to grow and develop professionally in their work. They want to develop themselves to their fullest capacity as creative and unique individuals. This is the concept of self-realization or fulfillment that many psychologists have noted as having a profound effect on what people do to achieve their ultimate goal in life. The Pittsburgh study indicates that when people can realize their hopes and ambitions in the work they do, they like their work, derive pleasure from it, and enjoy a high level of satisfaction with their jobs.

2. There is a group of five other significant factors that operate in the opposite direction, that is, that lead people to be unhappy and dissatisfied with their jobs. These are unfair or unsatisfactory administrative practice, supervision, compensation, and working conditions. These factors have little to do with personal growth of individuals. Instead, they are associated with the conditions that surround doing the job. They act to make the job environment unsatisfactory to peo-

ple, and hence they bring about feelings of dissatisfaction.

3. The two groups of factors—the satisfiers and the dissatisfiers—operate more or less independently of each other and in different directions. The satisfying factors lead people to feel good about their work. The other factors lead in the opposite direction, that is, to dissatisfaction with the job.

This was a new idea at the time. Until this study was made, the generally accepted notion was that any factor that affected people operated in a straight line. Thus, if poor working conditions caused people to become dissatisfied with their jobs, the presumption was that improved working conditions would cause people to become satisfied. But the study does not show this to be true. All one can say is that if working conditions are improved, people's dissatisfactions may disappear, but we still do not get much in the way of satisfaction with the job. Likewise, if the satisfying factors of achievement and recognition operate to make people feel good about their work, the lack of these factors does not (i.e., did not) lead to dissatisfaction. We can summarize this by saying that satisfying factors affect job attitudes mostly in a positive way, whereas dissatisfying factors affect job attitudes mostly in a negative way.

Performance Effects

We may recall that one of the questions the interviewers asked was, "How did this incident (good or bad) affect the way you did your job?" This information they got from the employees was not put in terms of exactly how much more or less they produced. Rather, what they got was an account of the effect on their performance—whether they worked harder and produced more, or whether they quit trying and produced less. In a nutshell, the results, then, were:

1. In about three out of four of the accounts in which the employees felt good about their job, an improvement in performance was stated as a result of their better feelings about

the work. The investigators list some of the statements made, indicating that the employees started working harder, more effectively, longer hours, with greater enthusiasm, doing part of the work at home, and so on. Furthermore, many of these effects lasted for a long time.

2. In about half of the accounts in which the workers felt unhappy about their jobs, a decline in work performance took place as a result. They said that they put off doing things, did not care whether the work got out or not, were not able to work as they had before, quit trying, slowed down, and so on. Here also, many of these performance effects lasted a long time.

There were various other effects. In about half the stories about unsatisfactory events, the employees told of thinking about quitting, or of taking steps to quit; some actually did quit. Clear evidence appeared that loyalty to the company, or organization, varied with the degree of job satisfaction. When the workers felt good about their work, they felt better about the company, and vice versa.

It is worth charting these effects:

I Satisfiers lead to	II Dissatisfiers lead to
Increased interest	Decreased interest
Increased enthusiasm	Decreased enthusiasm
Increased productivity	Decreased productivity
	An *increase* in quits

This chart summarizes results that are of considerable importance to supervisors. The increases in group I are almost exactly what any supervisor hopes for and tries to get in a unit. The decreases—and the increase in quits—in group II are the things that he or she hopes to avoid. Here is a direct relation between motivation and performance effects. If supervisors could set the satisfier factors into operation, they might expect the results in group I. If they could block or nullify the operation of the dissatisfiers, they might expect fewer or none of the results in group II. These are exciting prospects.

Finally, our investigators found no differences in the effects reported either by accountants or engineers or in different age groups or job levels. In other words, attitudes about work are probably true of people in general, regardless of their age or salary or the kind of work they do.

The investigators noted that there have been many contradictory reports with respect to the relation between morale and productivity. They suspect that this may be so because previous studies may have confused the factors found in the good and bad sequences of this particular study.

Later Studies

A whole series of studies followed the one made by Herzberg and his associates. One after another these investigations confirmed the findings of the original Pittsburgh investigation. The evidence, indeed, is now overwhelming that the Motivator-Hygiene theory[3] is essentially correct.

The original study included only two hundred workers, which was a small sample on which to base a theory about people in general. By this time, however, more than twenty thousand people have been involved in similar studies. Included within this number were people working at more than sixty distinctly different kinds of jobs. Some fifty studies were made by a number of psychologists and physicians, some of whom used Herzberg's methods and some of whom used other approaches. This last point has significance, indi-

3. The theory is often referred to in this way. The satisfier factors were called motivators. The dissatisfiers were called hygiene factors in a sort of parallel to medical hygiene, meaning preventive medicine and having to do with keeping an environment healthful.

cating as it does that the results were not necessarily associated with methodology.

The later studies included a sizable number of women as well as men. They dealt with skilled and unskilled workers as well as professionals. One study included more than one hundred Negro workers. And some included Scandinavian and Hungarian workers; these were conducted by Herzberg himself. His more recent efforts were aimed at workers in the Soviet Union, and first indications were that results would be the same there as in the United States, Scandinavia, and Hungary.

It is worthwhile listing at least some of the many kinds of workers studied. They included:

Scientists (chemists, physicists, mathematicians, and others).
Supervisors (foremen in a number of industries, managers).
Engineers (general, chemical, ordnance, aeronautical).
Accountants.
Extension agents.
Unskilled workers (food, engineering, and maintenance services).
Nurses.
Women executives.
Air Force officers.
Nonsupervisory personnel (in a variety of firms and government agencies).
College students.
Automobile assembly-line workers.
Women assembly-line workers.

In some of the studies, findings also showed that the theory applied to people regardless of their age, sex, salaries, educational background, personality characteristics, and of course, the kind of work they were doing. This was additional confirmation of the original study.

All this leads to the conclusion that a supervisor can rely on the Motivator-Hygiene theory with confidence.[4]

Putting the Study Results to Use

The conclusions of the Pittsburgh and later studies coincide remarkably well with experience. Supervisors readily agree that no matter how fairly people are treated, and no matter how pleasant their working conditions, they do not actually do their best until they have the freedom to show what they are capable of doing. And this in turn takes challenging tasks, full responsibility, and recognition of successful work, not only by a pat on the back but by actual promotion.

As we have already noted, the concept of supervision in the study appeared to be somewhat restrictive. As we use the term in this book, supervision includes everything a supervisor can do to bring about the greatest possible combined effectiveness of the people in getting work done. Thus supervisors must consider not only how they can eliminate job dissatisfaction, but also, and perhaps more importantly, how they can bring about job satisfaction. They must see what they can do about both kinds of factors, those that produce negative effects and those that produce positive ones.

In the material that follows, we consider the ways in which supervisors can make it possible for the factors of the Pittsburgh study to operate to best advantage. There are some over which the supervisor has almost full control, some that will come into play according to the initiative of the supervisor, and some over which he or she can exert little or no control. As we review these matters, we must note that there are tremendous variations in the policies

4. Many of the later investigations discussed here are portrayed in detail in *Work and the Nature of Man,* by Frederick Herzberg (New York: World, 1966).

and administration of different organizations, whether industrial or business concerns, and also among government agencies.

The Satisfiers

Several general points must be made at the outset. The Pittsburgh investigators noted that the factors operating in a negative direction—the dissatisfiers—form a sort of base on top of which the satisfiers can operate. This implies that until job dissatisfaction is eliminated, one can scarcely expect the satisfying factors to exert their fullest effect. Perhaps this is so, but possibly only to a limited extent. All experienced supervisors are aware that the challenge and stimulation of the work itself, plus responsibility, achievement, and recognition, can often outweigh low salaries, unsatisfactory policies, and poor working conditions. Many teachers teach because they love to teach; they will tolerate a great deal in order to keep on teaching. Similarly, many people in the government service, church organizations, business, or industry are there because they believe in the work they are doing—despite handicapping factors of one kind or another.

A second general point is that supervisors usually have it within their power to put most or all of the satisfier factors into full operation. This is in contrast to the negative dissatisfiers, over which the supervisor can ordinarily exert much less direct control. It should be obvious that no supervisor can press a button and cause workers to jump in response. What *is* possible, however, is for almost any supervisor to arrange things so that (1) the satisfier factors can operate, and (2) the dissatisfiers are minimized.

We review the satisfiers, then, in a slightly different order than they appear in the study. We do this merely to make our points easier to review. For each factor we consider the question: What specific things can a supervisor do to make it possible for the factor to motivate people as fully as possible?

1. *The Work Itself*

Three important possibilities seem obvious with respect to this factor. The first is that supervisors must make a real and convincing effort to be sure their people understand the importance of the work they do. Their job—whatever it is—relates in one way or another to the larger purpose of the organization. In turn, this larger purpose may relate to the welfare of the community, to the service of the public, or an important segment of the public, to the good of the nation itself, or, indeed, to the benefit of humanity—all this depending on the organization. Thus jobs can be shown to be closely and directly related to this broader purpose. It is true that many may not seem to be, and that routine, simple tasks may seem indirectly related indeed; but it is not so much a matter of the immediate job as it is the effect of that job on the broader purpose. The supervisor should not make this sort of thing ridiculous. No use trying to fool people into thinking they are important when they are not. But there is a legitimate bit of salesmanship here that a supervisor must think about. He or she is well advised to reread the short section on Principle One in Chapter 2; it bears on this point.

The second specific thing supervisors can do is rearrange the work performed by their unit so that each job is made as interesting as possible to each person concerned. So much depends on the nature of the work that it is hard to be specific here. However, in order to arrange things so that people will find the greatest possible satisfaction with their work—and thereby become more productive—we must go to some lengths to avoid the boring, the repetitive, the monotonous tasks that conspire to make work uninteresting and even downright unpleasant. Industry is facing this kind of a question; there is doubt about the productivity of people on the production line compared with their productivity in restructured, challenging jobs.[5]

Third is the question of whether people are placed in the best job for *them*. Personnel people talk about this as "placement." If the placement is poor, an individual may fail to find the job interesting and challenging. The question—to both the workers and supervisors—is whether a person might be more effective and productive in another kind of job than the one he or she finds lacking in challenge. We will assume here that the two points above have been tried, but that restructuring the job or explaining its broader purpose has no effect. Then a supervisor had better help the person look around for work in which he or she can find an interest. Doing this raises problems, to be sure. But too many people manage, somehow, to work out their whole lives at jobs they really do not believe in, do not care about, and would leave if they only could see their way clear.

2. *Responsibility*

Letting this motivating factor operate is well within the power of nearly all supervisors. There are three concrete possibilities.

The first, and for many supervisors the most difficult one, is to refrain from supervising too closely. Oversupervision tends to stifle initiative. Let people work! Give them the freedom they must have if they are to show what they can do. By such means, people's sense of responsibility for their work can be sharpened.

The second thing a supervisor can do is to assign workers more responsible tasks to perform. With this assignment, the supervisor again refrains from watching people too closely. Workers must be put on their own insofar as the work per-

5. Industrial and government supervisors alike will find it worthwhile to read Douglas M. McGregor, *The Human Side of Enterprise* (New York: McGraw-Hill, 1960).

mits. Here the supervisor is trying to build the sense of responsibility each worker should have.

The third specific thing a supervisor can do to develop more responsible people is to utilize the principle of participation discussed in the latter part of Chapter 6. As people come to share in solving the unit's problems and in helping make decisions, their sense of responsibility deepens. This has been proved beyond question by supervisors experienced in using the participative approach in the work of their units. It amounts to a sharing of responsibility for what is done.

3. *Achievement*

This factor is next because it is more likely to become completely effective after the two factors above are in full operation. With full responsibility for an interesting job, a person can be expected to try to bring it off successfully. The opportunity to achieve has to be carefully created. With this in mind, a supervisor can do such specific things as these:

First, study the work and the people with a view to providing opportunities in which they can attempt to achieve results. If at all possible, these opportunities should be such as to make the people extend themselves. They must have a chance at a task as creative in character as possible. If they can meet the challenge, the pride of achievement they experience will be for something more than the ordinary.

Next, the supervisor must encourage people to attempt doing something they may not quite believe they can do. By every appropriate means, the supervisor must urge and lead them on. The supervisor should be careful to avoid "whipping up the horses"; what is wanted is to get people to see that they have the opportunity, responsibility, and ability to tackle the task.

Finally, the supervisor must get the recognition factor to work as quickly as he or she sees people successful in performing a difficult or challenging piece of work. Achievement without recognition is somewhat like apple pie without cheese. The pie is good in itself, but the cheese helps make it just a little bit better.

4. *Recognition*

The operation of this factor, as we have just noted, is very closely related to achievement. In fact, it is seldom dissociated. Whatever people achieve—either a specific thing or a long-continued and sustained effort—recognition ought to be prompt and clear. Nothing in any rule or regulation of any government agency or industrial concern prevents a supervisor from recognizing the good work of people. In fact, of all the responsibilities a supervisor has, this one is more easily exercised than are any others. It is indeed a cardinal principle of supervision, as we noted in Chapter 2. Specific ways in which a supervisor can give recognition are listed under Principle Three in that chapter. All of them depend, however, on the premise that he or she first learn to recognize achievement on the part of people when it occurs.

5. *Advancement*

Here we have the only motivating factor among the satisfiers over which supervisors may not be able to exert full control. On the other hand, they can have about as much to do with its operation as anyone else, and ordinarily it is they who must set it in motion. Specific actions leading to activation of this factor should be these:

To start with, train the people for more responsible work. (This idea is discussed under Principle Five in Chapter 2, and in Chapter 10 on training.) The supervisor must also do all he or she can at this point to encourage people to improve themselves. All of this is aimed, of course, at preparing people for advancement. The training and the way in which people discharge greater responsibilities must, of necessity, be put in the record, that is, in the personnel folder. This is part of the preparation for advancement.

Second, recommend the people in the group who are well prepared and ready for advancement. If they make good, the recommendations will gradually gain weight. If they do not, or if only a few do, later recommendations will lose weight. The supervisor simply must make sure that recommended people can make the grade. This means, of course, that he or she must be assured all along that the records of accepted and discharged responsibilities are well founded.

We might add, by way of summary, that if a supervisor can set these five motivating factors into full operation, he or she has a better than average chance of developing a group of employees who find great satisfaction in their work. It is likely that these factors may outweigh the dissatisfiers, which we discuss in the following section.

The Dissatisfiers

In this group of five factors leading to job dissatisfaction, two are fully within the control of supervisors. These are the two kinds of supervision outlined by the Pittsburgh study—technical and interpersonal. This entire book is concerned with the many ways in which a supervisor can improve supervision. There would be little point in repeating them here, except to note that supervising is itself a job to which one has to apply the greatest possible intelligence. It is a thinking, planning, studying, analyzing kind of work. It is as challenging as any other kind of work we have. Those who do not understand or believe this should, without doubt, get into some other kind of work that will give them greater personal satisfaction.

There are a number of complicating problems associated with the activation of the other three factors, at least insofar as supervisors are concerned. These—policy, salary, and working conditions—most supervisors do not control, except in small part. Their efforts with respect to these factors must of necessity have to do with influencing others to help bring them into full operation.

1. *Policy and Administration*

The Pittsburgh study mentioned personnel policy in particular. This policy is rarely or never set by individual supervisors. Rather, it is stated by or emanates from the board of directors plus the managing heads of a company; in the federal service, it is set government-wide by the actions of Congress, the president, and the Office of Personnel Management. In both industry and the government, personnel policy is importantly influenced in one way or another by the action of unions. Sometimes the policies may be stated in writing; sometimes they may be no more than a body of unwritten principles based largely on precedent. But no personnel policy, written or unwritten, is any better than the administration thereof. If any policy is successful, it is because supervisors make it so. The policy is in their hands to make of it what they can or will.

Of key importance with respect to personnel policy is the need for a career system in any organization. Some businesses and industries have excellent systems, and some may have none at all. In the federal government, some agencies or bureaus likewise have excellent systems, and again, some have none at all. Political scientists have pointed this out before,[6] noting that true career systems and policies occur more or less as islands in the federal service. Supervisors in one of these—just as in the outstanding industrial organizations— are fortunate; they may operate accordingly. Supervisors not

6. The interested reader will find a very full discussion of this in the *Federal Government Service: Its Character, Prestige, and Problems*. Report of the American Assembly (New York: Columbia University Graduate School of Business, 1955).

on one of these islands can only try to reach shore by continually urging their organization to develop—and really implement—all aspects of a true career system.

Thus, while individual supervisors are in no position to set personnel policy, they can undertake to be as fair and enlightened in their supervisory practice as it is possible to be. Within whatever organizational climate they may enjoy, they can develop a small climate of their own, in their own units, in which it may be possible to eliminate a large part of the dissatisfaction that might otherwise occur.

2. *Salary*

With respect to this factor, as well as the one above, the supervisor can do relatively little except to see that government-wide or company-wide policy is carried out as well as possible. Pay scales are rarely set these days by individual supervisors. They may, of course, act with a union to foster the best possible wage and salary administration. But this is not action as a supervisor; it is action of a union member.

As between government and industry, salaries and wages tend always toward a balance. If at one time government salaries lag behind those of industry, at other times they exceed them. If there is a sizable discrepancy between salaries of similar positions in government and industry, a series of factors operate gradually to equalize them. At any given time, great capital may be made of observable differences, but given time, such differences are quite likely to disappear.

In any event, in either industry or government supervisors have the opportunity, indeed the responsibility, for seeing that positions under their control are properly compensated for the work performed in them—under whatever system they may operate. In the government service this means that they must understand how jobs are classified, what classification standards and specifications are, and something about how they are applied. They need not become a classification analyst themselves, but they should be able to discuss classification problems intelligently with such analysts. This is not to say that they should simply be adept at arguments or that they should be skilled at "blowing up" job elements. Rather, on the basis of their knowledge of classification, they should be in a position to recognize new or additional elements that may affect the grade of their job. And they should call prompt attention to these changes. If they do not get the grade they hoped for, they should make it their business to see that their people understand why. Their explanation should, in all fairness, omit reference to the so-and-so who classified the work.

3. *Working Conditions*

Most supervisors are in a sort of halfway position with respect to this factor. They can do a great deal to make working conditions reasonable. But there may be some working conditions they can do little or nothing about. Organizational units tightly packed in their offices for lack of space may wait a long time for the new building. Air-conditioning may be hard to get. Lighting may sometimes be slow in coming. Location of the office may not always suit most employees, and transportation may be horrible, as it is in many of our big cities.

On the other hand, within the facilities available supervisors can do quite a little. They can generate a friendly and businesslike atmosphere; make the most of the office furniture; watch the safety and health hazards and reduce them; and enlist the participation of their people in solving problems with respect to working conditions in ways on which they all can agree. And then they can continue to press for improvements. The knowledge that the boss is trying often helps to make poor conditions tolerable.

Some Concluding Thoughts

This chapter is a little different from most of the other chapters in this book since it is based entirely on the results of scientific studies. Also, it goes into greater detail. I wanted it to be an example of what we might have in every aspect of supervisory work if we had sufficient scientific research on which to base the most enlightened supervision possible.

From the standpoint of practical application, the reader should understand that there has already been widespread application of the Herzberg theory in both industry and government. It has been used as a basis for personnel programs, training programs, management development, and recruitment. It has been used in morale surveys, quality control, wage and salary administration, and job enlargement. Supervisors in both government and industry have been shown how to use it, and top management groups have used it to nullify the operation of the dissatisfier factors. The skillful application of this theory to management has been generally successful.[7]

For reasons such as these, as well as those already discussed, supervisors everywhere will do well to consider how they might apply these ideas to their own particular situations.

7. A full discussion of the remarkable results achieved at Bell Telephone is to be found in *Motivation Through the Work Itself* by Robert N. Ford (New York: American Management Association, 1969). See also M. Scott Myers, "Who Are Your Motivated Workers?", *Harvard Business Review,* January–February 1964, pp. 73–88, for an account of the use of the Herzberg theory at Texas Instruments.

8

Prejudice and Supervision

In the everyday operation of supervision we have been rely-ing on a considerable amount of prejudice—and there is a lot of this not only in our own society but in numerous other societies as well—whether the belief is that women are infe-rior to men, or that older people are inferior to younger peo-ple, and so on. Yet very few if any differences have been shown between the performance of workers from these vari-ous groups.

Although sexual identity ought not to play any special part in management or supervision, the fact is that it has, not only in the United States but also in most of the rest of the world. Perhaps the status of women is much better in our country than it is in China, Japan, or India, for example. Even so, we have a long way to go, although we have made a fair start.

Yet for all the attention that has been paid to such impor-tant legislation as equal opportunity for races and genders, one group of people are still discriminated against, often without legal or other protection. They are human beings sixty years of age or older. At the last census there were more than thirty-five million men and women in this group. There is an enormous wastage here of resources. In a thoughtful article in the *Personnel Journal* a long time ago,[1] J. W. Taylor, personnel director, noted:

> The more mature man has the tenacity, will power, and persistence required for creative achievement; he has the stuff to decide, start, stick, and finish. . . .
> The mature man's richer background of experience is immeasurably advantageous in the special work of problem-solving.

The *Personnel Journal* prefaces Taylor's article with the statement that "one of the most baseless, damaging, and wasteful beliefs in our country is found in the notion that the significant creative output of the nation comes only from its youth." Taylor's article gives numerous examples; Noah Webster wrote his monumental dictionary at age seventy; Socrates gave the world his wisest philosophy at seventy; Mark Twain turned out two successful books at seventy-one; Voltaire did his best work between sixty and eighty-four; Benjamin Franklin wrote his masterful appeal to Congress for the abolition of slavery at eighty-four; during the panic of 1933 Chief Justice Holmes was advisor to the president; at the time he was ninety.

One day we may have scientific evidence about all this. Today we must argue largely from experience, just as we must do insofar as women are concerned—and insofar as the next groups are concerned.

The supervisor will encounter members of numerous other groups who have suffered prejudice unfairly at work. There are the twenty-six million black people whose forefathers were the only people serving as slaves in America—the land of the free. There was a long struggle to achieve freedom, which came in 1865 with the 13th Amendment. But then, segregation prevented these people from playing on public golf courses, or seated them in the rear of

1. "Now, About Old Dogs/New Tricks," November 1968, pp. 786–788 and 810.

buses or the last, upper seats of theatres—and made it difficult for them to become qualified for society's best jobs. In the last several decades, the social oppression of blacks has been mitigated, but corporate America still has a long way to go to establish truly nondiscriminatory treatment.

Somewhat different aspects of discrimination, exceedingly difficult to measure, have to do with (1) prejudice operating against people from one place or institution by people of another place or institution, and (2) prejudice operating against strangers. The latter operation leads to the so-called buddy system, in which an appointing officer has a tendency—sometimes quite strong—to appoint people he or she knows rather than a stranger. In this instance, of course, there is a sort of "double-digit" discrimination, since the stranger may come from another state, place, university, or company. How to cure this type of discrimination cannot be specified. Every case is somewhat or completely different. But any appointing officer is well advised to think again before appointing someone.

The human mind is the power that thinking scientists and managers alike have stated repeatedly to be the most valuable moving force on earth. We have no scientific evidence that would enable us to differentiate between humans of different races, skin colors, religions, languages, or cultures. In Japan, as Servan-Schreiber puts it, the principal problem is one "of finding new areas to challenge each person's mind." It is a similar problem worldwide.

Recently I picked up a handbill from a table in the Department of Housing and Urban Development offering free materials to the public. This was originally issued by the United Technologies Corporation (UTC) of Washington, D.C., and published in the *Wall Street Journal*. It is, says the UTC, a twenty-five-year policy of the corporation to utilize handicapped people, wherever possible:

ANYTHING YOU CAN DO THEY CAN DO TOO

While you flex your muscles in front of your morning mirror
and congratulate yourself on your nimble brain, consider this:
The light over your mirror was perfected by a deaf man.

While your morning radio plays, remember the hunchback who
helped invent it.

If you listen to contemporary music, you may hear an artist who
is blind.

If you prefer classical music, you may enjoy a symphony written
by a composer who couldn't hear.

The president who set an unbeatable American political record
could hardly walk.

A woman born unable to see, speak, or hear stands as a great
achiever in American history.

The handicapped can enrich our lives.

Let's enrich theirs.

9

Insights into Human Behavior

For a number of years behavioral scientists have been studying the factors that motivate people. Maslow,[1] for example, developed the interesting and useful concept that the needs of human beings are organized in a series of levels. At the very bottom are needs for sheer physical survival—for oxygen, food, water, sleep, shelter. Next above them are safety needs—for protection against threat or danger. Above these are social needs—for belonging, for friendship, association, love. And on the top level are the egoistic needs—for self-confidence, achievement, knowledge, and for status, recognition, and the appreciation and respect of others.

Maslow's idea is that the physical needs of a human being must first be satisfied before he or she can think about much else. People devote all the attention required to getting enough to eat, to drink, or to protect themselves from the elements. Once these needs are satisfied and they are no longer hungry, or cold, or thirsty, their behavior begins to be motivated by needs for safety. When they were hungry they may have got food under conditions of extreme hazard. But with plenty of food, they think twice before risking danger. They are now motivated importantly by their need for protection from it.

1. A. H. Maslow, *Motivation and Personality* (New York: Harper & Row, 1954).

Generally speaking, once the lower-level needs are met, the higher levels become increasingly important as motivators of behavior. Thus it is that in our relatively affluent society, supervisors find their people motivated most commonly by egoistic needs—at the top level—and to a lesser extent by the social needs. Physical and safety needs are pretty well taken care of.

Now note that the egoistic needs are essentially the same as the satisfier factors developed by Frederick Herzberg. It could be said that the Herzberg and related studies have provided strong support for Maslow's theory, certainly insofar as the top-level, egoistic needs are concerned.

Theory X and Theory Y

A few years before Herzberg's study first appeared, Douglas McGregor published his now famous theory X and theory Y.[2] His ideas correlate well with the findings of Herzberg and with Maslow's theory.

McGregor pointed out that there are two contrasting points of view about how to manage human beings in an organization. The usual point of view embodies such ideas as these:

1. Most human beings dislike work and will avoid it if they can.

2. They have little or no ambition, dislike responsibility, and prefer to be led.

3. They are self-centered and are indifferent to the needs of the organization.

4. They resist change and want security above all.

5. They are not very bright, and they are easily misled by demagogues.

2. Douglas M. McGregor, "The Human Side of Enterprise," in *Proceedings, Fifth Anniversary Convocation of the School of Industrial Management, Massachusetts Institute of Technology,* Cambridge, 1957. Also under the same title in book form (New York: McGraw-Hill, 1960).

These beliefs about human beings are widespread, McGregor thought. They form the basis for management in many organizations. They influence managerial action in a major way. It is management's responsibility to organize and operate the enterprise. To do this it uses money, materials, equipment, and people to produce goods or services. This must be done efficiently if the enterprise is to be successful. In order to get people to work as well and hard as possible, management has to take a strong hand. It must direct people's activities, persuade them, reward them, punish them, control them. All this has to be done in order to get people to do what the organization wants.

This whole set of beliefs and assumptions, and the style of management based on them, McGregor has called theory X. But, as he said, this theory of management by direction and control is failing in our present-day society. It does not provide for the effective motivation of people whose physical and safety needs are satisfied, and whose social and egoistic needs are therefore dominant.

Obviously, we need a better understanding of human nature than is to be found in the theory X assumptions. McGregor used the findings of many behavioral scientists, including Maslow. Later he pointed to Herzberg's motivational theory as supporting a whole new set of assumptions about human behavior. This new set he called theory Y.

Theory Y consists of a series of ideas or assumptions that are strongly supported by the findings of scientists in recent years. These assumptions are as follows:

1. Human beings don't necessarily dislike work. They may enjoy it, or they may not. If the work is a source of satisfaction to them, they will perform it willingly. If not, or if it is a source of punishment, then, of course, they will avoid it.

2. Direction, control, rewards, and threat of punishment are not the only means to get people to work for organizational goals. Human beings will work hard and well to achieve objectives they believe in.

3. The satisfaction of egoistic needs (for achievement, recognition, self-confidence, etc.) can come about as people work toward these objectives that they have adopted.

4. Under the right conditions, the average human being wants and will seek responsibility. (Remember the Herzberg satisfiers.)

5. Imagination, ingenuity, and creativity are characteristics that most human beings, not just a few, possess. By and large, McGregor notes, people don't get the opportunity to display such characteristics in modern industry. When they do, the industry benefits.

What management has to do, McGregor felt, is to arrange things so that management and the people can work together for the success of the enterprise. He called this the principle of integration. It was stated in other words by James Lincoln in 1914 when he said that if he could get all the employees to want the company to succeed as badly as he did, there ought to be no limits to what they could do together (as noted on p. 69). What he did, in fact, was run the company in such a way that the people in it could achieve their personal goals best by working for the success of the company.

As most of us know, however, the practices of the Lincoln Company have not been widely adopted. McGregor did not feel that his theory Y would be widely or readily adopted either. The trouble is, management goes on thinking in terms of theory X. And it may be a long time before management is utilizing fully and widely the ideas in theory Y. But organizational operation is moving in the direction McGregor thought it should. Where this is taking place, remarkable results are coming about. The people in the organization are being encouraged to develop and use their knowledge, skills, abilities, and imagination to help reach the objectives of the organization. They do this because the company's objectives are theirs also. And in working toward these objectives the people find deep satisfaction in their achievement.

System 4

Beginning in 1947 the Institute for Social Research at the University of Michigan began studying the human problems involved in management. Rensis Likert, director of the institute, headed up the studies. In 1961 he published a summary of findings[3] and a new theory of management based on scientific research. More recently he has added to his original theory and supplied additional proof of its usefulness.[4]

Likert describes four different kinds of management systems:

System 1 he calls exploitive-authoritative. This system resembles closely the style of management based on the ideas and assumptions of McGregor's theory X. Threats, punishment, control, and direction are characteristic. The workers feel no responsibility for the organization's goals and do not participate in decisions. Managers don't trust their people and the people don't trust the managers. The workers are supposed to do as they are told and they usually find ways to resist or oppose management. Employees generally are afraid or reluctant to express their ideas about the work.

Systems 2 and 3 grade between 1 and 4. System 2 is the benevolent-authoritative system, a little better than system 1. System 3, the consultive system, lies between 2 and 4. It is better than 2, but not as good as system 4.

System 4, which Likert calls the participative system, stands in greatest contrast to system 1. It resembles closely the style of management based on the ideas and assumptions in McGregor's theory Y. Under this system people at every level feel a real responsibility for the organization's goals and they work hard to reach them. There is real participation throughout, and the people help in making important deci-

3. Rensis Likert, *New Patterns of Management* (New York: McGraw-Hill, 1961).
4. Rensis Likert, *The Human Organization: Its Management and Value* (New York: McGraw-Hill, 1967), and with Jane Gibson Likert, *New Ways of Managing Conflict* (New York: McGraw-Hill, 1976).

sions. Managers have complete confidence and trust in their people, and the people reciprocate. There is complete freedom to express ideas about the work.

In discussing the four systems, Likert points out that the theory X ideas implicit in system 1 must give way to theory Y ideas if system 4 is to become operative. There must also be much greater use of the motivational forces of self-actualization, i.e., more use of Herzberg's satisfiers. Greater participation must be practiced. Better communication must be made possible both up and down.

The close parallel among the findings and thinking of Likert, Herzberg, Maslow, and McGregor is apparent. And there are dozens of other behavioral scientists who, in one way or another, have come forward with findings that support the work of these four.

Likert, however, using some simple but ingenious methods, has been able to relate productivity to his systems. He uses figures for the most part from industrial concerns, but he has a few from government units also. He and his associates have now shown conclusively that the nearer the management system is to system 4, the more productive the organization is. But this is not all. System 4 management results also in lower costs and higher earnings. It results in better union relations and fewer strikes and work stoppages. And it results in better worker attitudes and higher morale.

Conversely, of course, the nearer the management system is to system 1, the lower the productivity, the higher the costs, the lower the company earnings, the poorer the union relations, and the lower the morale.

Likert believes that with more scientific facts a still better system could be developed. Right now, system 4 is clearly the best we know how to achieve. But when we know more, we may have a system 5 or 6 that may help us to do even more.

There is little question that system 4 takes more knowledge and skill. It may take several months for a supervisor to learn. It also requires that the entire top management of an organization consciously and deliberately undertake to foster it. Likert believes it takes up to a year to prove to all the people that the system (1, 2, or 3) is really changing (to 4). Only when the entire organization is convinced, do the results begin to show up. Once under way and used with skill, system 4 can produce results previously impossible.

Is it possible to change a manager? The whole top management of an organization? Likert cites actual examples showing that it can and indeed has been done.[5]

McClelland's Work

In the meantime, at Harvard other work has been going on which offers considerable promise. David McClelland, director of the Center for Research in Personality, and his associates have been studying the whole question of achievement for the past twenty years.[6]

He notes that some human beings are challenged by opportunity and feel impelled to work hard to achieve something. Most human beings, though, are apparently much less interested. McClelland thought it might be possible to develop the desire to achieve in people who apparently had very little of it.

It was found, to start with, that people with a strong need or desire to achieve exhibit such characteristics as these:

1. They set goals for themselves that they have to stretch a little to achieve. The goals are not impossibly high, nor ridiculously easy. But they are a challenge to excel.

2. They set goals like this only if they can personally influ-

---

5. A work by Alfred T. Marrow entitled "The Failure of Success," published by Amacom, a division of the American Management Association, New York, 1972, offers additional and important examples, well worth reviewing.

6. David C. McClelland, "Toward a Theory of Motive Acquisition," *American Psychologist,* vol. 20, pp. 321–333, 1965. Also by the same author, "That Urge to Achieve," in *Think,* November–December 1966, pp. 19–23.

ence the outcome by doing the work themselves. They don't like to gamble, because they don't like to leave the outcome to chance.

3. They enjoy the work itself and are most concerned with their personal achievement. They work not so much for the rewards of their success as for the success itself.

4. They prefer work in which they can get concrete readings on how well they are doing. They want to know their score, so to speak, as they go along.

The reason why some people act this way is that they habitually spend their time thinking about doing things better, McClelland says. It appears that they don't inherit this trait; they get it from the way their parents work with them as children. The parents set moderate goals for them, then are warm, encouraging, and nonauthoritative in helping them reach the goals.

The Harvard scientists can determine this need for achievement in people by some simple tests. People with high scores—that is, with a high need or desire for achievement—get promoted more rapidly, make more money, and in general do better than do other people.

McClelland and his associates more recently have been trying to find ways of developing this need for achievement in people. They have developed a course in which such training is attempted. They have, he notes, put everything into the course that they feel may help to change people. And in a number of cases, the course has produced highly satisfactory results.

Executives from a number of companies in America and in India and Mexico have taken the course. Two years after completion, careful statistical studies showed that the people who took the course had done much better than comparable groups of people who had not. The executives expanded their businesses faster, made more money, were promoted faster, displayed greater initiative in new ventures, and so on.

The Mexican executives were an exception; reviews of their activities did not show them to have developed greater need for achievement as measured. In other studies, the Harvard scientists had difficulty with students from low-income groups, although they were successful with medium-income students. They are not sure yet exactly why this is so, and a great deal more research may be required in order to find out. But they are working hard to develop the techniques. After all, as McClelland himself states, they have "a tremendous potential for contributing to human betterment."

Here again let us note some interesting interrelations. Maslow classified the needs of human beings, with egoistic needs, including the need for achievement, at the top level. McGregor developed theory Y, aimed at satisfying the egoistic needs. Herzberg showed that several of the egoistic needs are of key importance as satisfiers and that achievement is one of the key motivators. Likert discovered system 4—a system of management dependent largely on satisfying egoistic needs. He said theory Y is essential to such a system. And finally McClelland appeared very close to finding out how to develop in people the need for achievement that may lead to greater success.[7]

Literally hundreds of years of effort have gone into the research of these behavioral scientists. Now we are witnessing a breakthrough in human motivation that may well change the world in which we live.

7. For further highly interesting reading about these developments, *Motivation and Productivity,* by Saul Gellerman, is recommended (New York: World, 1966). This book is well written and easy to read.

10

Training

One of the most challenging responsibilities any supervisor faces is the task of providing the proper training for the people supervised. Supervisors can scarcely expect top performance if the workers' knowledge or skill is not up to the demands of the work they must do. The better trained the people are, the more productive they can be, both individually and collectively.

Now it is obvious that any employee working at a job gains experience, that is to say, he or she learns. To put this another way, an employee is taught or trained by the experiences in which he or she participates. These experiences may be accidental, in which case the training proceeds no faster than the experiences happen to occur. Or these experiences can be planned and arranged in such a way as to provide for steady, directed development of knowledge and skill. In both situations people learn, but in the planned situation they have the opportunity to learn much more rapidly and correctly.

Training is the process of teaching, informing, or educating people (1) so that they may become as well qualified as possible to do their work, and (2) so that they may become qualified to perform in positions of greater difficulty and responsibility. Training has to be a two-way process. Someone must teach; someone must learn. Obviously the problem of training is the age-old problem of learning, or education.

Ordinarily we may think of education as the formal part of the learning process, which takes place in school. By training we usually mean that part of the learning process devoted to developing proficiency in a particular job or in a particular organization. When we train someone, we usually have in mind a very specific objective, attainable in a relatively short time, in contrast to "education," which is ordinarily much broader in scope and longer in development.

There are several schools of thought with respect to methods of training:

1. There is the sink-or-swim school, the members of which believe that the best way to train people is to throw them into the work situation and let them sink or swim. In the University of Hard Knocks, they will tell you, the successful person will have learned, and learned well, what it takes to perform the job.

Learning by trial and error alone is usually considered a crude and wasteful way to learn. And yet the lessons learned by experience, as we say, seem to be firmly implanted in one's mind. We may be scornful of the method, even appalled at the waste it involves; yet we cannot deny the depth of the impressions resulting from it. Its principal drawbacks are its slowness and its waste of effort. As a device for introducing people to their jobs, it can be improved principally by stepping up its rate and reducing its waste. We cannot afford a lifetime to get a person into full operation on a job. But before we discard the method because of its extreme slowness, or because of its waste, we should certainly capitalize on its virtue—that of making deep and lasting impressions. If we can retain its virtues and correct its faults, the trial-and-error method of training can be of value.

2. Then there is the "send-him-out-with-Joe" school, the members of which believe that the best way to train a man or a woman is to put the individual under the wing of an ex-

perienced employee who will show the individual the ropes and teach all he or she needs to know. This is the age-old apprenticeship system.

Properly used, this method can be a successful one, but unfortunately it is not often used skillfully. If Joe, the experienced worker, is a good teacher or trainer, and if he is really interested in training new people, and if he has enough time to devote to training (instead of production, which is his normal job), the apprenticeship approach can be valuable. Frequently enough, however, Joe is not a good teacher, and worse, he may resent being stuck with a new person. Joe, in fact, may be far more interested in doing his own job than in training new recruits. This last situation may be so because Joe is in a competitive situation, working against other experienced people in similar jobs to turn out the most and the best work. All this is equally true of women.

At any rate, this method has more to recommend it than the sink-or-swim method. It is generally somewhat less costly than that method, and it is likely to train people more rapidly.

3. The third school is the systematic school, the members of which believe (a) that training should be planned, scheduled, and systematically carried out; (b) that it should be based on the needs of the individual in relation to the demands of the job; and (c) that the best-known methods of teaching should be selectively used as they may apply.

There may be some of the apprenticeship method used, and in certain situations, a little of the sink-or-swim approach. But they will be used, along with many other methods, only where they are judged or have been found to be the best possible ways to get certain points across.

It is this systematic approach to training that can get the job done for the lowest cost. However, because of the variation in needs, plans, and people, such an approach can easily become overly elaborate. The impulse to add frills may prove almost overwhelming. And when this happens, supervisors may, in a revulsion of feeling, conclude that perhaps the old methods are best. This conclusion will be a natural one, however erroneous.

Kinds of Training

For our purposes, we may conveniently classify the many kinds of training into four general categories. Every supervisor must devote adequate attention to each of the four:

1. Orientation training.
2. Job or production training.
3. Maintenance or refresher training.
4. Career or developmental training.

These four kinds of training merge freely into one another, and there is no particular virtue in trying to keep them meticulously segregated. Still, the training process ought to be undertaken in a certain order, and any supervisor ought to be aware of this sequence, as follows:

1. *Orientation Training*

This type of training is aimed at acquainting the new employee with the organization, his or her place in it, and the part he or she is expected to play in its work.

When new people start to work in an organization for the first time, they are eager to know what sort of an outfit it is, what they are supposed to do, whom they will work with, and the like. The desire for knowledge and receptivity to training are possibly greater at this particular time than they may ever be again. Both men and women know they are ignorant, so to speak, and the career of each depends on the acquiring of knowledge and skill. The new person feels great need for being shown what to do and how to do it. He or she is likely to be more attentive, more open-minded, and more eager than the experienced employees, who have already learned their work. What the new man or woman learns in the earliest days in an organization is likely to remain indelibly fixed on his or her mind. People on the verge of retirement often refer to their first days in the organization, which seem to stand out clearly in their minds, even after the passage of many years.

Orientation training is needed, without exception, by every new person who enters an organization. It is intended to *orient* the new employee, and the subject matter must include such things as are shown under supervisory Principle One on page 116. Orientation training is one obvious method for a supervisor to use in carrying out responsibilities in supervision.

Note that we said *every new person* entering an organization should be oriented. We stress this point because people in many agencies and companies seem to feel that a new clerk or messenger or typist should be trained only for particular duties. These people do not understand the difference between a job and *the start of a career.* Nor do they realize that people work for more than the money they are paid. For people to become real and enthusiastic workers for their organization, they must know something about it, and feel a sense of pride in being part of it.

It is worth noting here too that orientation training in many government agencies and in many companies is performed by a training officer or staff in special training classes. But this cannot relieve the supervisor of any responsibility whatever for the training of his or her own people. The new trainee may learn a great deal in the training class. But no such class can provide personal details that orient the new person in a particular job, in a particular group of people, with a supervisor, and in the unique work situation to which the person is assigned. Any supervisor must instruct the new people in such matters, preferably ahead of any orientation training class. Furthermore, it is of considerable importance that the supervisor check carefully to be sure all new people understand clearly what they were supposed to have learned in the training class.

2. *Job Training*

This type of training is aimed at teaching employees how to do the job for which they were hired. The intent is to get employees into full production in their jobs as soon as possible. For this reason, such training has often been called "production training." Its objective is to instill full understanding and knowledge of the job and to teach trainees *how* to perform all those activities that make up the work they are expected to do.

Job, or production, training is often mishandled. Frequently this comes about because a supervisor does not have clearly in mind either the objective of such training, the need for speed, or the best methods to use. Job training is by no means a simple matter, nor is it something to be handled by any single method. We can illustrate the situation by the following ideas.

Training costs money. *A completely untrained employee is the most expensive employee on the payroll,* since he or she is paid for practically no production at all. When such employees are at last fully trained, they are, as we say, *earning* their pay. All during the time they were not producing as fully as a well-trained person should, the cost of what they *did* produce was higher than it would have been with a trained person.

The first day new people report for work, they cannot earn their pay. They must learn all about their jobs and how to do them before they can fully earn the salary attached to their positions. Thus, from the time such employees first enter on duty until just before they are finally producing fully in a job, they are actually not earning a full day's pay. Only after they are fully producing are they worth the salary paid them.

We can show this situation in a simple diagram, thus:

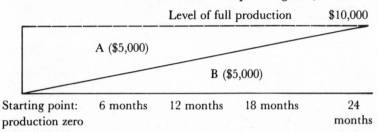

Untrained employees start at zero; they produce nothing. Gradually they may learn by experience how to do the work involved in their job. Twenty-four months after they started to work, they have reached "full production"—that is they are performing productively in all the duties they are expected to undertake. At the halfway point of twelve months, they are producing about half of what they will produce in another twelve months.

The triangular segment marked B represents the production of the employee. The segment marked A represents the area of no production. In other words, if, as the diagram shows, it takes the person two years to become fully productive, then the *total* production of that person during the two-year period is about half of what it would have been if the person had been fully trained to start with.

New employees earn about half of the salary paid them during the two-year period. The other half they do not earn. If their salary were $5,000 per year, then the cost to the organization employing them to get them into full production is $10,000 in two years. In this same period, learning employees earn half their salary, or $5,000. The other $5,000 goes for experience, or for their learning.

Suppose it were possible through systematic, intensive training to reduce the learning period in our hypothetical situation from twenty-four months to twelve. Our diagram would then look like this:

It is obvious on inspection of the diagram that area A has now been reduced in size (actually it has been cut in half), and that areas B and C together represent the productivity of the new person in a two-year period. In this situation the individual is now earning three-fourths of $10,000, or $7,500; and there is a loss of only $2,500 (in area A).

To put this another way: we can obviously well afford to spend up to $2,500 on such employees' training, *if we can get them into full production in one year instead of two.* The less we have to spend, of course, the greater the profit we can hope to make. For example, $500 spent on training could get us a net profit of $2,000 in production. If the training cost is $1,000, the net profit is $1,500 in increased production. Thus we may conclude that the lower the cost of intensive training, the greater the profit to be realized in terms of the productivity of such employees. It should be clear, too, that *we must spend money on training to realize this profit,* and that if no money is spent, we lose the production anyway.

We would do even better if we could get such employees into full production in six months. In this case we could afford to spend up to $2,500 plus $1,250 (half of A above), or $3,750, on training. Each time we cut in half the time it takes to train them fully, we are able to spend one-half plus one-fourth, plus one-eighth, etc., of the annual salary. Note, however, that as the training time becomes shorter, the amounts we realize from speeding up the process become smaller.

The more intensive the training, the more difficult it is for employees to absorb it. There are practical limits to the learning ability of people. Many jobs require as much as two years for employees to learn them. Most of these can be learned through intensive, systematized training in half that time, or possibly in one-fourth that time. Other jobs may take much less time to learn. The learning time for every job actually varies with the kind of job it is; each job requires study to determine the amount of time.

To illustrate what all this might mean, suppose we take an organization of ten thousand people with a yearly turnover in personnel of 10 percent. In such an organization there would be a thousand new people each year to train. Let us suppose that the average learning time for a new employee is one year, but that with intensive training we would have the employee in full production in six months. If the average salary were $5,000, then we could afford to spend up to $1,250 per person for job training. This would amount to $1,250,000 for a thousand people per year. This amount is far in excess of what it need actually cost for the training. In such an organization as this—which is a reasonably common example—a possible profit of considerable size could be realized from such a training venture.

At any rate, it is clear that even though we consciously spend no money on systematic training, the learning period will cost money anyway. The amount is proportionate to the length of time it will take most people, on the average, to learn their jobs. The higher the salary a person gets, the greater the cost, or loss. It is possible to overspend on job training. A little analysis of training costs and results can often help reorient the program.

Supervisors must undertake job training with considerable care. Careless or indifferent handling of this training can result in far higher costs than are necessary. Worse, it can result in employees lacking adequate training for their jobs. No organization can afford to use exclusively the philosophy of the sink-or-swim school, or the send-him-out-with-Joe school of thought. Nor is there too much truth in the belief that a person must be "seasoned," or left a long time in a job to "gain experience." The fact is that properly planned, skillfully handled instruction can turn out a well-trained employee *at a rate at least equal to the rate at which the individual can learn.* If, by seasoning, we mean primarily the development of wisdom in action, or improved judgment, then the constant application of trained intelligence to a variety of new problems can bring this about. This, too, can be planned and arranged.

3. *Maintenance, or Refresher, Training*

Training of this kind is aimed at keeping people up to date, as well as enabling them to brush up on knowledge they have already received. Involved here are new ideas, information, methods, techniques, and developments, as well as reviews of older materials and ideas. Such training is needed both to help keep employees at the peak of their possible production and to prevent them from getting into a rut.

Refresher training takes place after job training has been pretty well completed. The objective here is literally to maintain knowledge levels. Too much refresher training can be wasteful, of course, but the need for its judicious, periodic application is clear. In one sense, the introduction of new ideas is not strictly refresher training in the proper sense of the phrase. That is why "maintenance training" is perhaps a better term.

Involved here too is the need for stimulating employees to undertake their own self-improvement. If they have learned to continue their own education, they will be a far easier subject for maintenance training (and for the career training outlined next). Unfortunately, not all high school or college graduates have learned how to go on learning. Frequently enough, a supervisor must undertake to create in people the desire for learning and for improving by their own efforts.

4. *Career, or Developmental, Training*

This kind of training is devoted to developing and improving the knowledge, skills, and abilities of the employees, so that they may ultimately perform work of greater responsibility than their present position entails. Such training is not necessarily related to the immediate job. Rather, it is designed to broaden employees' knowledge and experience, and it may involve periodic testing to determine whether they have arrived at a point where they can accept and discharge responsibilities and perform in a position of greater difficulty than the one they started with.

Such training as this is difficult to come by in an organization that does not have a fully developed career system. It is relatively easy under a good career development policy. Even so, it requires thoughtful study by any supervisor of people—their abilities, ambitions, interests, and potentialities.

Here we come up against the idea that an employee may, as we say, reach a "ceiling." We mean by this that we think an individual can go no farther, having developed as far as one is able. No more career for that person, at least vertically; the person's limit has been reached. And yet experience indicates that such an idea is so frequently untrue as to be a fallacy, more often than not. Too many people who (their supervisors thought) had "reached their ceiling" have gone on to much greater work and reached unsuspected heights in different and more challenging situations. Possibly the supervisor could not make the job challenging enough.

In career training, as in maintenance training, but to a much greater extent, there is need for stimulation of employee self-improvement. Career training becomes increasingly important as a man or woman learns the job and does the work with increasing confidence and ease. An employee can be provided with opportunities, but in the end it is the individual employee who must make the most of them. Obviously, the person who is prepared will make more out of an opportunity than one who is not.

Some Principles of Training

There are some half-dozen principles any supervisor must know and understand if training responsibilities are to be dealt with adequately. These principles, or important ideas, are listed below, as follows:

PRINCIPLE ONE

People must be interested in learning before they will accept training.

If employees are not really devoted to their work because they enjoy it, training them is more difficult. Moreover, the experienced people may feel that no one can teach them anything about their job, and that no one knows about the work as well as they do. Such individuals are often quite hard to train.

There are many reasons why people may become interested in learning. Some develop a love of knowledge for its own sake. Some are continually eager to learn because they are ambitious, because they believe in the organization for which they work, because they take pride in accomplishment, because they desire recognition for outstanding work performance, because they want to earn more money, or for many other reasons.

There is always the additional spur of the realization that the boss wants certain things done. If it is not clear that the boss expects the people to be able to do a certain thing as a result of training, then possibly only their good-natured willingness is the motivation.

PRINCIPLE TWO
Training must be suited to the individual needs of those being trained.

Before teaching or training people to perform any kind of work, the supervisor must evaluate what the people can already do and what they already know. Once it is clear what the particular deficiencies are—and this is a highly individual matter—then a training program can be devised to help correct these deficiencies. What we do is to fit the training program to the person instead of fitting the person to the training program. The training must be related to the job that must be done and to the performance standards for that job.

PRINCIPLE THREE
Training must be done either by a supervisor or under a supervisor's direction.

A supervisor may personally teach people or may arrange for someone else to do so. However the job is done, the supervisor cannot escape the personal responsibility, inherent in the supervisory job, for being sure the people *are* well trained for their work.

This is part of the basic philosophy underlying all supervision. If people are to look to supervisors for guidance and direction, the supervisors had better be there when they are needed. They must see that the new employees learn their jobs, and that they are given every possible opportunity to grow in stature, so that they may undertake increasingly difficult work. If training is conducted by another person or by other means, without reference to the supervisor, trainees tend to grow away from their supervisor. They become obligated, as it were, *not* to the supervisor but to the outside source of their enlightenment. Always, any person must understand that however the training and development may be carried out, the supervisor is the person who planned it, arranged it, or gave it. An experienced and able supervisor, intent upon commanding the respect and loyalty of the people, will always be found closely associated and identified with their development.

A training officer cannot be made responsible for the training that should be conducted by the supervisor. The training officer properly has the job of helping and advising the supervisor on needs, methods, arrangements, and evaluation of results.

PRINCIPLE FOUR
The rate of training should equal the rate at which an individual can learn.

This principle would seem particularly applicable to new employees. After all, nothing is to be gained by proceeding at a snail's pace when it is possible to go forward more rapidly. In fact, the slower the rate of training in relation to the learning ability of an individual, the more wasteful it is. Capable teachers will tell you that some students learn faster than do others, and that those who can learn rapidly deserve special attention. So it is also with new employees. The sooner they can achieve full productivity, the sooner they earn their full salary, and the sooner the organization stops losing money while they learn.

But this principle is equally applicable to career training. Every job in a company or government agency becomes vacant, sooner or later, and often unexpectedly. The more people there are who are ready to assume greater responsibility, the more likelihood there is that the vacancy will be filled with a qualified person. In large organizations particularly, the number of positions of responsibility available may often become somewhat greater than the supply of well-trained people. Thus career training conducted at a rate consistent with learning ability is not only advisable but necessary.

PRINCIPLE FIVE
People can learn by being told or shown how to do work but best of all from doing work under guidance.

There are those who can "talk" a good fight. And it is frequently said that "book learning cannot substitute for experience." Experience, we say, is the best teacher. But experience can be misleading, too, if it is the wrong kind, so that careful guidance of experience would seem to be wise.

What the principle leads to is the idea that while oral instruction or demonstration can reduce a period of trial-and-error fumbling, in the end the person being trained must actually perform the job. It is during performance that he or she actually learns what must be done in order to continue performing successfully.

PRINCIPLE SIX
Training should be planned, scheduled, executed, and evaluated systematically.

It may be that we have several principles here, all combined into one, but since the process of training ought to be continuous, we may consider these four phases together.

1. *Planning.* As has already been implied, a training plan should contain a list of the ideas and skills that are essential to the job for which people are to be trained. In addition, it should indicate the approximate time required, on the average, for the total training. In making such a list and timetable, it is important to avoid either oversimplification or overelaboration of the training items. It is possible to subdivide the list into a series of ideas or skills so detailed in

character as to obscure the essentials in which training is needed.

Obviously, a general plan can be made for any job without reference to an individual employee. It is when the listings are compared with the employees' skills and abilities that the plan becomes significant for any given individual.

2. *Scheduling.* Tentative completion dates should be indicated for each item in the training plan. These dates should be set after due consideration of the total time ordinarily required and of any seasonal or other factors likely to affect the schedule. The schedule can later be adjusted to fit the rate at which any employee learns.

3. *Execution.* As the training plan is carried out, the trainer or trainers can use the plan, including the schedule, as a checklist. Appropriate notes can be included on each item, indicating satisfactory completion, need for additional work, and the like.

4. *Evaluation.* Failure to evaluate the results of training is possibly one of the commonest of all faults of training programs. It is not enough to *give* the training, however well planned, scheduled, and conducted. *In the end we must ascertain whether the training was successful.* Workshops, conferences, or training meetings aimed at improving employee understanding or performance simply cannot be evaluated by asking the participants how they liked the session. The question is actually not whether they found the conference interesting, boring, stimulating, or tiresome. The question rather is: What did each participating employee learn? The employees may agree that it was a "splendid session," a "fine meeting," or "one of the best they ever attended." But *unless they learned* what was being taught, the session was a flat failure.

There are several direct ways of finding out what the trainees learned—that is, of evaluating the training. These ways are well known to teachers, as follows:

1. Oral or written tests are given to ascertain whether the trainees have learned what they have been told or have been

assigned to read. These tests need not be elaborate, but they should establish beyond doubt whether the trainees have the required knowledge of the subject.

2. Actual performance is observed by the trainer to determine whether the employees have developed the ability and the skill to do the required work. Obviously, the performance cannot be guided, nor should the employees be coached when the testing is going on. Guiding and coaching are used while teaching is going on. When people are being tested, they are on their own.

3. The work done by trainees is reviewed after a time (short periods at first, longer ones later) to check the quantity and quality of results. This type of evaluation ordinarily comes after items 1 and 2 above and continues thereafter as long as the employees stay in the position. Test results of all kinds can well be noted in the training plan.

Exactly how plans and schedules are made and executed and how training is evaluated are matters of choice with the supervisor. The important point is that the training job be done in a systematic way, with an objective clearly in view, and that its results be carefully checked upon its conclusion.

The Device of the Training Plan

At this point it is worthwhile to describe a simple working device that has proved generally useful to supervisors. This is a *written* training plan.

Supervisors who have never made one of these will find if they try it that their job will become much better organized. After all, it is difficult to keep in mind all the many things a new person must learn. It is much easier to jot them down in a list. And if the plan is developed *with the trainee participating,* the training itself tends to gain significance.

Such a plan can be developed in many ways. One useful approach is as shown below. Use a plain sheet of paper and head columns something like this:

1	2	3	4	5	6	7
Job or activity		Who will do the training	When it will be done	How	Where	Remarks
1.						
2.						
3.						
4.						
5.						

Inspection of this beginning page of such a plan shows how it may be used. Column 1 carries a complete listing of all the things a person must know and be able to do in the job being entered. This listing can be prepared for any job well in advance—provided the duties of the job are clear and well understood.

Column 2 is simply checked if the employee already knows or can do the specific item. If it is blank for any activity, then we use the next columns.

Column 3 carries the name of the person who will do the training. Supervisors can put their own initials here whenever they intend to do the training themselves.

Column 4 can indicate conveniently the dates when the training will take place. Or a single date can show the deadline by which time the item should be completed, e.g., "by June 15." And the year should be shown.

Column 5 should show how the training will be done. The entries might read: "conference," "reading assignment," "on the job," and the like.

Column 6 shows where the training will take place. For example, a training conference might be held in Denver. An on-the-job bit of training might be done in the "office."

Column 7 is used to indicate that training on any item is

completed satisfactorily—or that additional training is needed. If the latter is true, it can be added at the end of the list, for renewed effort.

This plan is developed with the trainee personally, and is given to the trainee to keep. *No copies* need be made.[1] As the training progresses, the supervisor asks trainees to bring in their training plan and appropriate entries are made on it. Additional items will probably have to be put in the plan—which thus becomes open-ended. Experience in various organizations suggests that such a plan has a useful life of perhaps as much as two years. After that, keeping it up may become somewhat of a chore. Experience also indicates that formalizing this plan—on a printed form, with copies to various places—tends to diminish its value. Nor does it need to be typed.

Training Methods

There are many ways to go about training people that vary with the student and the teacher. No one can say generally that one method is better than another. The question is how effective the method is with the people being trained. Listed below are some of the better-known methods as suggestions for the consideration of supervisors.

1. *Assigned Reading*

This is most useful in connection with a job requiring knowledge that must be utilized for performance. Assigned reading would ordinarily be somewhat less useful with simpler work—for example, filing or message-carrying. Even here, however, assigned reading can be useful in giving employees an explanation of the agency in which they work and

---

1. If you don't like excessive paperwork, don't make it!

the importance of their task in relation to the whole. As always, the trainer must ascertain by testing whether the employees understand what they have read.

Reading is also essential for maintenance and career training, and it is one of the important devices used to broaden the horizon of people as they develop. Professional people cannot keep up to date in any field or increase their knowledge and perspective without extensive reading. This has become increasingly true as the world's knowledge has grown, and as books, journals, and magazines have been published in constantly growing quantity.

A person's reading must necessarily change with the jobs. If, for example, he or she begins a career as an engineer, it is appropriate to read material on engineering. But should the person become a supervisor, then that individual should turn to the best that has been written in the fields of supervision, management, and administration. All too frequently, the technician-turned-administrator fails to realize the extent of the literature available in a new field of effort. This literature requires as much searching, selection, and study as does that in any technical field.

2. *Individual Counseling and Guidance*

This method of teaching includes techniques usable by a master and apprentice or by a tutor and a student. But as used in job training, for example, it may possibly include something more.

In the first place, supervisors (trainers, in this case) must observe their people in the performance of their work. In doing this, they make mental or written notes of the things the trainees do that need improvement.

Second, trainers should discuss the observed performance fully, commending the good things and suggesting ways of improving items that are in need of it.

Third, and later on, they should again observe the

trainees' performance to ascertain whether the suggestions have been taken up and used.

This simple three-step procedure is capable of considerable variation. For example, rather than *suggest* an improvement, supervisors may *demonstrate* by performing the work themselves. Also, in situations where a supervisor is guiding a number of people, he or she is well advised to take written notes on the suggestions made, keeping a copy and giving one to a trainee. This is simply for the purpose of reminding the trainer (and the trainee) later on of what the suggestions actually were. Where many trainees are involved, it is quite easy to confuse both performance and suggestions unless they are committed to writing.

3. *Group Training*

This method of approach presumes that all the people in the group need or want to be trained in the same thing. For example, a half-dozen new recruits all need to know about the organization they have just joined. In this case, the group method is obviously appropriate and is less time-consuming for the teacher than is covering the same ground with each person individually.

The reason why there are classes in any school is that a great many more teachers would be required to deal with each student on an individual basis. Instead, one teacher is able to talk to a class, develop discussions, undertake demonstrations that can be observed by all students at once, and test what has been learned by questioning or observing later performance. Even in the classroom, however, the teacher must devote as much time as possible to each student individually. When the ratio between teachers and students is large, the individual attention per student may be small— sometimes so small as to be unsatisfactory, at least for certain students.

In recent years a great deal of material has been published

on conference methods, some of which has value for supervisors who are undertaking maintenance training with their group. With due allowance for some of the unimportant frills that have crept in, supervisors can profit by a study of the general principles of holding conferences. Possibly one of the most important of the techniques suggested is that of gaining participation in discussion by *all* members of the group. This technique is simple and, indeed, requires only thoughtful observation on the part of the chairperson, but it is often neglected.

The leader of a group being trained must make use of various visual aids. Blackboards are obvious. Large-sized pads of paper are especially useful if a record must be kept. Pictures, photographs, slides, motion pictures, flannelboards, tackboards, recordings, and other devices may also be used where they are needed. But the devices should be kept commensurate with the subject matter. It is worth recalling that the greatest teachers the world has ever known had none of these.

11

Communications

Almost every day supervisors have to make themselves understood by their people, and almost every day they must try to understand what their people are attempting to convey to them. This two-way process is usually labeled *communication,* and a great deal depends on it. If supervisors and people cannot or do not communicate very well, the work they must perform will suffer accordingly. This need for communication is not confined to the field of supervision; it poses the same problem in any field of endeavor. Wherever people are trying to do something together—build a bridge, run a government, or establish world peace—what they get done depends on how well they understand each other.

People have been *mis*understanding each other for a long time. Misunderstanding can easily lead to dislike, enmity, or hatred, and it has frequently led to war between nations. It is far wiser for supervisors to think carefully about their *own skill* in conveying and receiving ideas than it is to assume, without thinking, that they already know all they need to know about the subject.

There are two important ways by which people communicate, that is, convey ideas to one another. They do it by talking and listening. Or they do it by writing and reading. In both of these processes, one person sends a message and another person receives it. In both the processes, the sending and receiving require considerable skill.

The principal trouble in this matter of communicating is that so many people think it is really no problem at all. Talking and listening and reading and writing are usually thought of as things everyone knows how to do. And there is a certain amount of truth in this belief. However, each of these skills has to be studied and learned, and one does not necessarily learn them by going to school. Many supervisors have failed because they assumed that any or all of the following simple statements were true:

1. Anyone who talks plainly to another person will always be understood.

2. Anyone can listen to another person talking and easily understand the meaning.

3. Anyone can write what he or she means on paper, and the meaning will be understood by anyone else who reads it.

4. Anyone can read what someone else has written and understand what the writer meant.

All these statements are dangerous generalizations. They are not "trick" statements, nor are they intended to contain any "hidden" meaning. All assume perfectly ordinary situations involving the language we use every day. The statements imply that talking and listening and reading and writing are usually quite simple skills you learn more or less as you grow up—at home, in school, among your friends.

It is dangerous, however, to take these four skills for granted. Many books have been written about language—its uses, weaknesses, and deceptions. The interested supervisor may find it worthwhile to review some of these books, which treat the subject more fully than we can do here.[1] For our

1. S. I. Hayakawa, *Language in Thought and Action* (New York: Harcourt, Brace, Jovanovich, 1949); Stuart Chase, *Tyranny of Words* (New York: Harcourt, Brace, Jovanovich, 1938); Stuart Chase, with Marian Tyler Chase, *Roads to Agreement* (New York: Harper & Row, 1951); and Alfred Korzybski, *Science and Sanity* (Lakeville, Conn.: International Non-Aristotelian Library, 1958).

purposes, we will discuss four aspects of communicating in a way that may be most practical for the supervisor. The four aspects are that a supervisor:

1. Must be able to speak clearly.
2. Must be able to listen.
3. Must be able to write clearly.
4. Must be able to read with understanding.

Talking-Listening

Of the two skills involved in the talking-listening process, most people seem to have the greatest trouble with listening. They assume that listening is the same thing as hearing, and that anyone who can hear can therefore listen. (And it is true that if your hearing is impaired, you will have more difficulty listening than a normal person will.) But listening as we are using the word here requires not only that you hear but also that you understand what you hear. To do this you must *think about* what you hear another person say when the person is talking to you. Actually, your speaker may not be skillful at all in getting ideas across.

The key to successful listening is to be an active, *demanding listener*. The idea is that you try as hard as you can to be sure you understand correctly what a speaker is trying to tell you. This means that you cannot be thinking of what *you* are going to say as soon as your speaker pauses for breath. Instead, you think about your interlocutor's meaning. This takes some effort if you have not tried it before—and many people have not. We are often so anxious to get our own ideas across that we try to do all the talking and hence we miss what others want to tell us. We must devote our *whole* attention to the business of listening.

Now it happens that scientists have developed some valuable and important ideas about listening. This has been done notably by psychologists and by specialists in general semantics, which has to do with the relation between language and human behavior. The semanticists suggest that there are three key questions a good listener should keep in mind while listening to a speaker. We list them first and then discuss each one.

1. What does the speaker mean, i.e., what is the speaker trying to say?

2. How does the speaker know, i.e., what evidence is given?

3. What is the speaker leaving out?

1. *What Does the Speaker Mean?*

Several ideas are important to bear in mind here. In the first place we must realize that the meaning of the speaker is *not* in the words used. You simply cannot assume that words are used exactly the same way that you use them. The meaning is in the speaker, not in the words. Start your listening therefore with the idea that you do not know what the speaker's words mean to the speaker—and you must spare no pains to find out. Probe. Ask questions: "Do I understand you to mean?" "Is this what you are saying?" "If I understand you correctly, you mean." Tell the speaker in your own words what you think is meant in order to find out whether you understood correctly.

It is important to check your understanding when the speaker is using what we think of as ordinary, simple words that are nontechnical. It is usually safe to assume you understand correctly when a speaker uses a technical word—providing you know its meaning. For example, if the speaker talks about sodium chloride, you may be sure that the speaker means table salt, since sodium chloride is the chemical term for table salt—and *it has no other meaning*. But for the commonly used words there are many meanings. For example, if I tell you that I saw an interesting tie the other day, you do not know whether I am talking about a necktie, a football game, a tie on a railroad track, or something else.

We are told on good authority that the five hundred most-used words in the English language have a total of some fourteen thousand meanings, as listed in the Oxford English Dictionary.

2. *How Does the Speaker Know?*

This question does not imply that you should take a challenging position with the speaker. Instead, you must try to find out the basis for what you are being told. You must look for the facts, the evidence, behind what the speaker is saying. You must ask more questions: How did you learn this? Why do you say this? How do you know? Can you show me?

You ask such questions diplomatically, after your speaker has finished. What you want, remember, is to understand what the speaker means. To help you do this, you are trying to discover how correct and how factual the statements are.

3. *What Is the Speaker Leaving Out?*

It may occur to you at this point to wonder how you can possibly listen for something that is not spoken. And here we have an important difference between hearing and listening. You cannot, of course, hear what is not said. But as you listen, you may realize that your speaker is leaving a number of things unsaid. He or she may leave out important facts and details; may favor one conclusion when you can see that there are several others; and may not see or say anything about the implications of the conclusion favored. All this takes work on your part. But remember, we pointed out in the beginning that successful listening cannot be passive; it must be demanding and, hence, active.

Some General Rules about Listening

In addition to the three questions a skilled listener must keep in mind and use, there are a few general rules that can also help the person listen. Most of these come to us from the psychologists. The rules are not difficult to observe, although they are widely neglected.

First of all, it is important to *relax* when you are listening. If you strain too hard, you are likely to find it correspondingly harder to understand. Extensive controlled experiments by the United States Navy during the Second World War with airplane personnel confirmed this idea, which had long been held by the psychologists.

These same Navy experiments showed, too, that a second general rule was important, a rule that the professional psychologists have been using for many years, especially since the time of Sigmund Freud. This rule is: *hear speakers out.* Let them talk until they are finished. Do not cut them off. Do not contradict them. Do not start looking out the window. Listen actively and carefully to what they say, all the way through. Then start asking your questions. This simple approach often has the effect of helping speakers say more plainly what they mean. To find listeners actually waiting until they are finished is likely to be flattering to them. They find that you seem *interested* in what they have to say, and they will work all the harder to be sure you understand their meaning.

This leads us to a third general rule, which embodies a familiar method of the psychologists. This is to listen patiently, without criticizing, passing judgment, or giving advice. The idea is to let a person speak as freely and fully as possible, without fear of censure or blame. This procedure is known to psychologists and psychiatrists as *nondirective counseling.* Listeners must be patient. They usually confine remarks to restating what the speaker has said, in slightly different words. This causes speakers to feel not only that they are being listened to, but that they are truly being understood. When speakers get through, you most specifically do not tell them you think they are wrong, or stupid, or foolish, or prejudiced—even if you think so. Instead, you go ahead using your three questions.

The fourth general rule is an interesting one. It is that in order to listen well, one must *disregard symbols of authority* as such. We cannot listen effectively if we are overawed or impressed by a speaker's title, name, rank, academic degree, uniform, wealth, or position. These things are not necessarily evidence that what the speaker is saying is reliable or valid. You evaluate the statements as usual, patiently hearing the speaker out, then using your three questions. In the words of Wendell Johnson, whose ideas we have been using liberally here:

> The quality of his (the speaker's) voice, the color of his skin, the slant of his eyes, his height, weight, and apparent age guarantee nothing with respect to the wisdom or foolishness of what he says. Truth can be lisped, stuttered, or twanged through the nose just as well as it can be molded by a meticulous Harvard or Oxford tongue. It can be mispronounced. It may be ungrammatical. Whether it comes in a satin case or a paper bag is a matter of no importance. To a general semanticist, the Men of Distinction are first of all, and often solely, just colored pictures. The art of listening involves realistic appraisal of the conventional symbols of authority, as such.[2]

The Other Half of the Talking-Listening Process

Let us now put ourselves in the position of the speaker. Let us assume that when we speak, our listeners are going to be active, demanding listeners, bent on trying to understand us. Now, what can we do to bring about the best possible communication? (We are discussing the way a speaker talks to one or two people, remember, not to a large audience.)

2. Wendell Johnson, "Do You Know How to Listen?", *Etc.*, Autumn 1949, pp. 3–9.

Clearly, we must *think about* our listeners and be just as active in trying to get our meaning across as they will be in trying to understand us. Our listeners will hear us out—so, we are as brief as the subject matter permits. We speak with care, choosing our words well, clarifying each point as well as we are able. Since our listeners will want the evidence for our statements, we take pains to provide it. We try for truth as objectively as we can. Our listeners will be watching for what we leave out, so we try for completeness in our statements from beginning to end. In every way possible to us, we try to think of our audience, that is, our listeners, and how likely it is that they are getting the meaning of what we are trying to say.

All this is no more than using the ideas about listening in reverse. But there are some other things we know that can help us when we are doing the talking. The same Navy experiments mentioned earlier also brought out some useful points about talking. They showed, for example, that speakers who talked too fast did not get across as well as those who spoke more slowly. This was especially true when the speakers were using simpler, more commonly used words. It helped also if speakers made a real effort to talk in short sentences, and to use patterns of inflection or tones of voice that would help to bring out meaning. From these experiments we can say that (1) speakers should avoid talking too fast, (2) they should use plain and simple words as much as possible, (3) they should speak in shorter, rather than longer, sentences, and (4) they should use the inflection of their voices to lend emphasis and clarity. Speakers cannot do these things unless they *think before they speak.*

Further help to speakers trying for good communication comes from Irving Lee. In his book *How to Talk with People*[3] he suggests a number of things speakers would do well to *avoid.* Some of these are:

3. New York: Harper & Row, 1952.

1. Try to avoid bluntly contradicting those with whom you are talking. You should be trying for understanding, not to make your listeners angry.

2. It is unwise to use inflammatory words or to descend to name-calling. If you say or imply that a person is a fool, that person is likely to get angry. If you call someone any kind of nasty name or otherwise insult the individual, you will usually get the same effect. This does not help communication at all; it only defeats it.

3. Try to avoid generalities whenever it is possible to be specific. For example, you may have had a bad experience with two women supervisors, but you cannot therefore generalize that all women supervisors are no good. You can, however, state that with two particular women supervisors whom you have observed, your experience was not good.

4. Try not to sound *final* in your statements. Put them on a tentative basis, and say or imply that you are still looking for a better conclusion. For example, if you say, "This is the *only* way we can do this," you may arouse more argument than if you say, "So far, this way looks pretty good, but possibly another way may have occurred to you."

5. Try not to talk down to your listeners. If you give the impression that you think you know all there is to know about a subject, your listeners may form the opinion that you are conceited or overconfident. This does not help understanding.

6. You personally, as a speaker, will do well to avoid becoming angry at your listeners. Likewise, you should avoid feeling that if a person disagrees with you that person is therefore either foolish or stupid. And keep in mind that when someone differs with you, he or she is not necessarily conducting a personal attack on your integrity.

7. Avoid using the hard approach rather than the soft approach. Introduce your critical or contradictory statements with such simple phrases as "I wonder if we could look at it this way ... You may be right, but would you be willing to

consider . . . ? You may know more about this than I, and I hesitate to say, but . . . I realize you have a very good point, although perhaps we might look at it this way . . ." Studies of arguments in conferences made by Irving Lee indicate pretty clearly that the "gentle phrase," or soft approach, tends to reduce markedly people's resistance to criticism. On the other hand, the blunt hard approach tends to ruffle the listeners' feelings—and agreement becomes more difficult to reach.

One of our ablest diplomats, Benjamin Franklin, had some things to say about the soft approach. He used it with great skill, and his *Autobiography* notes in one place:

> The way to convince another is to state your case moderately and accurately. Then scratch your head, or shake it a little and say that is the way it seems to you, but that, of course, you may be mistaken about it. This causes your listener to receive what you have to say, and, as like as not, turn about and try to convince you of it, since you are in doubt. But if you go at him in a tone of positiveness and arrogance, you only make an opponent of him.

The soft approach must be sincere. Lee's simple studies showed that this approach made some difference about two-thirds of the time. And he suggests that if you do not get results in a given situation, why not discard it for other methods?

The Writing-Reading Process

We are not concerned here with writing or reading literary masterpieces. Our intent is to discuss some simple ways of writing and reading that may help us in communicating with each other. No more. Anyone of ordinary intelligence who is able to read and write can learn these simple methods.

Many experts have worked on the problem of making

writing as readable as possible. All of them have approached the problem on somewhat the same basis. They have taken sizable groups of people and tested their comprehension of different types of written material. They ascertained what kind of writing was easily understood by people with a fifth-grade education, sixth-grade, seventh-grade, and so on, up through college. People who have graduated from grammar school, that is, the eighth grade, in general can read much more difficult material than can those who stopped their education at lower grades. High school graduates can read—with ease—more difficult material than can be easily and comfortably read by eighth-grade graduates. College graduates can do still better. On the basis of many years of study of hundreds of people and their reading comprehension, various formulas have been developed. These formulas can be used to classify most kinds of written material.

We use here a formula developed by Robert Gunning, a communications expert, in his book *The Technique of Clear Writing.*[4] His formula is not necessarily the best, but it is by all odds the simplest to use. The Gunning formula enables you to arrive at what he calls the "Fog Index." The higher the index, the more "fog" there is in the written material. The lower the Fog Index, the less fog there is. Gunning's formula offers a quick way to estimate how easy or how hard any piece of writing is. This is the way you use it:

1. Count off 100 words in the written material you want to test. Do not use a larger sample than this, because the formula doesn't work if you do. Make a mark at the end of the hundredth word. If the material is long, you will have to take several samples, say at every tenth page or hundredth page.

2. Figure the average length of sentence in the 100-word sample. Stop with the sentence that ends nearest (either before or after) the 100-word mark. For example, if two sentences make up 104 words, then the average sentence length

4. New York: McGraw-Hill, 1952.

would be 52 words. If there are ten sentences in 96 words, the average length is 96 divided by 10 or 9.6 words.

3. Next find the percentage of hard words. To do this, count the number of hard words—which Gunning calls words of three syllables or more—in the 100-word sample. (The word "next" has one syllable; "number" has two; "syllable" has three.) In doing this, do not count capitalized words, such as Paris, London, Congress, etc. Do not count words that are combinations of short, easy words (such as bookkeeper or white-collar). And do not count words that have a third syllable when *ed* or *s* is added to them (such as expected or refuses).

4. Last, do the figuring. Since we have a 100-word sample, the number of hard words can be used directly as the percentage figure. First, add the number of hard words to the average sentence length. Then multiply the sum by 0.4. This will give you the Fog Index. The factor of 0.4 relates the sum to school-grade reading level. You may take our word for it that the formula really works, even if you do not understand why. If you are interested in the theory behind the formula, read Gunning's book mentioned here.

Now let us apply this yardstick. We will take a piece out of a bulletin on supervision. We have underscored the hard words:

> There is need also for much additional basic and applied research: research to determine the major duties of supervisors' jobs, the differences among them, and the situations which help determine the qualifications needed, and to develop new methods for evaluation; and applied research to test the validity of new and existing selection methods on the supervisors of many different types of supervisory positions. Much more than half of the total research work reported here is based on supervisors of blue-collar workers, an important group, but far from being the only group for whom supervisory selection is important. The organization of.

Our line here stops us at the end of 100 words.

This passage contains 97 words through the sentence that ends nearest the 100-word mark. There are two sentences. So we divide 97 by 2 to get 48.5. All the words underscored add up to 22 hard words. (Note that we did not count report*ed* or blue-collar.)

Now we do our simple calculation:

Add	48.5	(Average sentence length)
	+ 22	(Hard words)
Total	70.5	
Multiply		
by	× 0.4	
	28.20	—The Fog Index

As it happens, there simply is no twenty-eighth grade in school. Our sample indicates that the writing would be hard to read for everyone, regardless of school education. The writer must expect to find that the readers will be few, and of these few, only a handful may spend the time and effort required to understand what is meant.

Before you smile at this example, better test some of your own writing—one of your letters, a memorandum, or something else you have written. Many people are shocked to discover that they habitually write with a Fog Index far above college reading level. Certainly a great many memorandums have a Fog Index of 20 to 30, which means that the people who must read them have considerable difficulty understanding them. Worse, when especially difficult memorandums are completely misunderstood—as they so frequently are—the activities involved may become very badly snarled. Test some of the instructional material you get from time to time. Test an article or two of the *Reader's Digest* or *World Press Review,* which scale their articles to reach large numbers of educated adults.

In the following table you can see how the Fog Index relates to reading level. The figures in the third column give the percentage of people in the United States who have reached the grades shown. For example, 88 percent of us have had at least an eighth-grade education, and we can read with ease any material with a Fog Index of 8 or less. Note that even college graduates can read such material with ease, not just grammar school graduates.

Fog Index	Reading Level by Grade	Percent of People Reaching Grade	Medial School Years Completed
17	College graduate	3.5	
16	College senior	9.5	
15	College junior	11.6	
14	College sophomore	16.6	
13	College freshman	21.0	
12	High school senior	53.6	12.1
11	High school junior	61.6	
10	High school sophomore	67.9	
9	High school freshman	75.0	
8	Eighth grade	87.8	
7	Seventh grade		
6	Sixth grade		
5	Fifth grade	96.1	

Younger people generally have had more education than have older people. And men generally have had a little more education than have women, except that many more women than men have had four years of high school.

Now we might get back to our sample and try making it easier to read. In doing this we are somewhat handicapped because we are not sure exactly what the writer meant. The writer could have done a much better job than we can do. Here is a rewrite, with the hard words underscored as before:

We need more research. We need to know the major duties of supervisors' jobs and how they differ. We must know what qualifications a supervisor should have for any given situation. We must learn how to judge these. We need to study how valid our selection methods are with supervisors, in many kinds of jobs. Most of the research reported here has to do with supervisors of blue-collar workers. This is an <u>important</u> group, but it is far from being the only group for whom <u>supervisory selection</u> is <u>important</u>.

As rewritten, the sample now contains 89 words. There are seven sentences, so the average sentence length is 89 divided by 7, or 12.7. There are 11 hard words, that is, 11 out of 89 words are three-syllable words. We divide 11 by 89 to get the percentage, which is 12. We apply our formula thus:

Add	12.7	(Average sentence length)
	+ 12	(Percentage of hard words)
Total	24.7	
Multiply by	× 0.4	
	9.88	—The Fog Index

If the rewritten sample correctly expresses what the writer had in mind (which we do not know), then the written material is now easy and comfortable reading for anyone who has finished two years of high school. As such, it would probably be read by far more people, with greater understanding, than our original sample with a Fog Index of 28.2.

Note, by the way, that we made no special effort to be brief. The rewritten piece happened to come out a little shorter than the original, but it might just as well have been longer. What we are saying is that ease of reading is more important than being brief, if brevity results in hard reading.

We may now draw some conclusions about communication by writing, based on the use of a Fog Index, as follows:

1. Just as speakers must try to express themselves as clearly as they can for their listeners' sake, so must writers do likewise for the sake of their readers. Writers have an even harder task because their readers cannot ask them questions about what they meant. They can only ponder what they wrote.

2. Supervisors who must write letters or memorandums— or who must sign material written by others for them—

should have some means of judging how readable they will be. Gunning's Fog Index is one way this can be done. Another excellent method is explained by Rudolf Flesch, and this one also deserves careful study.[5]

3. Because short sentences and simple words make reading easier, writers must *think about* that fact *as they write.* You will find, after a little practice, that you can indeed produce more easily readable material. But this does take conscious effort. It means also that when you write, you have two jobs to do. First, your subject matter must be correct. Second, the way it is written must be consciously scaled to the reading level of your readers.

A Note about Brevity

Many supervisors or administrators habitually demand that reports, letters, and memos be brief and to the point. "Give it to me in one page. Condense it to a single paragraph," they say. We can sympathize with such requests, because we may know that executives are busy and that there are many demands on their time. However, if you are one of these brief-and-to-the-point people, better consider whether you are getting what you really want. You just may be getting brevity at the expense of understanding.

For example, consider the following sentence. It is brief and to the point: *"Condensation diminishes comprehension."*

The Fog Index of this item is 41.2. (There are three words in the sentence. The percentage of hard words is 100—they're *all* hard words. Thus, $100 + 3 \times 0.4 = 41.2$.)

That sentence is harder to understand than the following: *"If you condense things too much, people will have a hard time understanding what you mean."*

The Fog Index of this item is 8.8. (There are 16 words in

5. Rudolf Flesch, *The Art of Readable Writing* (New York: Harper & Row, 1949). This book is a lot of fun to read. Furthermore, it's tremendously helpful to all who are trying to improve the clarity of their writing.

the sentence. The percentage of hard words is one in 16, or 6.2. Thus $16 + 6.2 \times 0.4 = 8.8$.)

Possibly the solution is to provide the hard-pressed executive with written material that is complete and understandable. But put a summary at the very beginning. If readers are interested in the summary, then they can read further, if they have time.

Some Ideas on Reading

We now come to consider the other half of the writing-reading process, that is, the business of trying to understand written material. In doing this we cannot do more than accord thoughtful and careful attention to it. There is no chance, ordinarily, to ask the writer what is meant. Of course, it is always possible to write a letter to an author or to the office the memorandum came from. This takes extra time, and sometimes you may not realize that you have misread the material. What we are emphasizing here is that when you *read* something, give it your full and critical attention. Think of the three questions you would ask of a speaker, restated as: (1) What does the writer mean? (2) What is the evidence for what has been written? (3) What has the writer left out? These may help you to understand what is on the page.

But there is far more to reading than the critical study aspect. So much material comes in printed or mimeographed form—books, bulletins, magazines, newspapers, memorandums, handbooks, manuals, letters, etc. Almost all persons trying to keep up with what is going on in the world, and in their own organization, are likely to get a little desperate about it. And there seems so little time to digest it all.

For slow readers the situation seems hopeless. They simply cannot seem to read fast enough to get through half the things they ought to. Or so they think. The fact is that people who can read rapidly were not born that way. They have *developed* their skill. All those who can read at all can learn to read more rapidly providing they are trained or train themselves to do it. What this takes is the application of a little common sense plus practice.

Sorting

The common-sense angle has to do with sorting out what you really *need* to read. Sorting is really an organized approach to reading. It is often more important to a busy person than an ability to read rapidly.

You most certainly do *not* need to read everything that happens to come your way, word for word. A great deal of written stuff is not worth your time. Some of it may be. So a few minutes spent sorting the wheat from the chaff can save you possibly hours of valuable time later on. As a suggestion, you can easily sort reading material into groups like these:

1. *The material you don't need to read at all.* This may include instructions that do not apply in any way to *your* work. It may include books or bulletins that are of no value to you. It certainly includes a great deal of material in any daily newspaper—all the classified ads, all the death notices, and so on. This is the kind of material that simply is not important to you. Best advice is to get rid of it as soon as you identify it. *But do not read it!*

2. *The material you may want to refer to later.* This is reference material. After you skim through it, you file it in some way so that you can put your hand on it when you want it. You do *not* read it until you *must.*

3. *The material you want to understand thoroughly.* As you are sorting and skimming through written material, you run across a few things that you decide are *really* important to you. *This is the real reading.* Read this material carefully. Reread it, study it, and spend the time it takes to learn what is in it. Chances are very good indeed that the amount of

material that comes to your desk that *must* be carefully read is far smaller than that in the two groups preceding.

There is probably another group of material that you may read for amusement or diversion. Detective stories are in this category, and so are the comics, magazine stories, and many novels. You may spoil these if you try too much system on them.

Rapid Reading

Your sorting process should cut down your required reading substantially. What is left may amount to less than 10 percent of all the reading material that comes your way. This figure does not mean much, of course, because it depends on an individual's interest and critical stance.

Even with the material you are going to read, there is still some sorting to do. It pays to read summaries first. It pays to skim the material, reading only the beginning sentences of the paragraphs. It pays to look at pictures, diagrams, and figures. In approaching this material you are still doing so with critical caution. Could be you do not have to read it after all; perhaps the summary is all you need.

With the final sorting done, you can afford to practice reading the material rapidly. As you try this, remember that *you cannot acquire a skill all at once.* You have to keep trying.

The trick in rapid reading is to see and comprehend *more than a single word at a time.* The more you can get at a glance, the faster you can read. With practice, you can eventually read a whole line at a time, or possibly more than that. Since many printed lines contain ten to fifteen words, what this means is that you may be able to read ten to fifteen times as fast if you are now a one-word-at-a-time reader.

One way to practice is to try to see and understand a phrase of several words at a quick glance. Look away from the page as soon as you have glanced at your group of words,

and think about what you saw. When you have decided
what the phrase meant to you, turn back and read each
word of the phrase. Was your idea correct? If not, try again.
If it was, try seeing a somewhat larger group of words. Try a
whole line once in a while. In the end it will come to you, if
you really want to learn badly enough to keep trying.

To many people, who are convinced that they simply cannot hope to read rapidly, all this may seem ridiculous. But
great numbers of people have nevertheless become rapid
readers through just this sort of process.[6] Progress may be—
usually is—slow at first. But the ability to read and comprehend rapidly is worth a great deal in these times when we
can learn so much from written material. It is possible, in
many cities and in many government agencies, to get short
courses in rapid reading. A supervisor really troubled by a
slow reading habit may find it worthwhile to find out where
he or she can get such a course.

The question really is, of course: What would it be worth
to you to be able to read ten times as fast—or even twice as
fast as you do now?

One last point must be made: some material *must* be read
slowly. Some people are able to read at a rate of six hundred
to eight hundred words per minute, but they cannot do this
accurately with a textbook on mathematics or Lincoln's
"Gettysburg Address." Thus the rate at which you read must
be properly adapted to the material. You alone can judge
this.

6. A good article expanding this subject is Carol and Roger Bellows, "The
Management of Learning," *Personnel Administration,* November–December
1960, pp. 19–26. "Speed Reading Is the Bunk," by Eugene Ehrlich, may
startle you. It was published in the *Saturday Evening Post,* June 9, 1962, pp. 10
and 16.

12

About Organizations

Every supervisor and his or her group of people are part of an *organization* of some kind. It may be small, perhaps consisting of only a few people. Or it may be large, consisting of hundreds, thousands, or even millions of people. It may be an organization of almost any kind—business, religious, governmental, industrial, medical, or some other. But whatever the kind or size, the organization, in one sense, is the house, the environment, the social system, the atmosphere, so to speak, in which the people work. For this reason, it is essential that supervisors know something about organizations in general and a great deal about the organization of which they and their people are a part.

An organization is a group of people working together to get a job done. This job is often given different labels. Some call it the "objective," others call it the "goal" or "aim," and it is often called the "purpose." The purpose is the thing we get together to do—to build dams, manage national forests, manufacture radios, or collect taxes. In the case of the federal government, Congress usually states the purpose of an agency in what is called enabling legislation. The purpose of many business or industrial organizations is not always to be realized so readily.

Accomplishing the purpose of an organization is not simply a gang job. For example, in a dam-building organization not everyone works directly at the job of building dams. Some of the people design the dams, some buy the materials, some run machines, some hire laborers, some keep the books, and some do other kinds of jobs. All of these are essential to the principal purpose of building dams. What we are saying is that each of the people in an organization has a certain part of the job to do, a part that is important to the whole purpose. Obviously, there has to be someone to lead or head the organization who is responsible for seeing that the purpose is achieved, that everyone plays a proper part, and that the whole operation is well managed. This is the leader, chief, or administrator. The part that he or she plays is of key importance to the work of the whole organization.

In a small organization it is possible for one person to perform many different tasks. In a larger organization these tasks may have to be divided up among a number of people, each doing a particular share of the job. And as organizations become large—still with a single purpose—a number of problems begin to appear that may seem unimportant in a small outfit. One of these problems is *coordination.* This is a broad term with many and often uncertain meanings. We use it here to mean *how we work together,* with all doing their part, and only their particular part, in such a way that we get the main job done as efficiently as possible and to the satisfaction of all concerned. This sounds simple enough, but coordination is often difficult to get.

Another problem of importance, especially in the big organizations, is the problem of communications. All the people must be kept fully and currently informed of what is wanted and what is going on. Unless they are all able to work at their task with full understanding, the organization as a whole may not work at peak efficiency, and the purpose may not be correctly achieved. Large organizations sometimes employ specialists in communications to help solve this problem.

The Line-Staff Organization

There are many ways in which people and their tasks can be arranged in an organization in order to get work done efficiently. But most government agencies are organized in what is known as a line-staff system, and so are a good many businesses and industries. This system has been in use for many centuries, and credit is generally given to military organizations for developing it into an effective working tool. You may find in books on the subject a definition that reads something like this: The line-staff system is a chain of organization units operating under authority delegated from a central source; and at various points in the organization there are groups of people called staff, whose function is advisory as distinguished from the function of command.

This definition is correct, even if a little obscure. Let us then illustrate a simple line-staff organization thus:

Leader
— Helper
People doing work

In this chart a leader is directing the work of four people, with the aid of a helper. The helper is the leader's staff. The staff helper does no directing of the four people, but only helps the leader. Putting this another way: the leader has the responsibility for seeing that the organization gets its job done; has the authority to see that it gets done properly; and has a staff officer to help. The staff officer could be, say, a bookkeeper who keeps the accounts, pays the workers, pays bills, and keeps track of profits or losses. The leader could probably do this alone, but we will assume he or she cannot look after everything and still get the main job done. So someone has been hired that the leader can lean on or depend on to keep the books. In these words we have indicated where the word "staff" comes from, for a staff is a stick or pole you use to lean on. A staff, then, supports you, and in our chart the leader leans on the staff helper, who supports or helps the leader by keeping the books.

When the bookkeeper begins to feel that he or she should have more to say about running this little organization, trouble can develop. The leader may tell the workers to do one thing, but the bookkeeper tells them it would be better to do something else. The workers get confused; they become uncertain and possibly do nothing at all. In this situation our staff helper has started giving orders, which is not what he or she was hired to do at all. Coordination is bad because not everyone is playing a proper part. Communications are bad, too, since there is misunderstanding about what should be done. In order to get the organization humming again, the leader must tell the bookkeeper *and* the four workers who alone will give the orders. The bookkeeper will give none; the bookkeeper's job will be to keep the accounts, pay the workers, pay the bills, and keep track of profits and losses. When everyone understands, the group goes to work again. Thereafter the leader keeps an eye on overly ambitious staff helpers and curbs any move on their part to assume command again.

Actually, of course, organizations are much more complex than this. But there is always a leader at the head of them: there are staff people who do special kinds of work; and there are workers who are doing the direct work on the main job. We can illustrate a more complex line-staff system like that on page 159.

In this chart, we can still see the leader, who goes by many names, depending on the organization: director, governor, chief, administrator, commissioner, superintendent, president, and so on. In this organization the head has a technical staff consisting, let us say, of engineers. The leader also has an administrative staff; here the people deal with problems of budgeting, accounting, personnel, contracting, buying, selling, renting space, and other problems of similar character. State directors have similar but smaller staffs to help with the technical and administrative problems in their state. Area directors have a similar setup to help deal with problems in their part of the state.

The main line in this line-staff organization runs from the administrator to the state director, to the area director, and finally to the operating units. This is what the military call the chain of command. This means simply that there is a chain, or line, of people in the organization who have the authority to give orders. The administrator gives orders to the state directors. None of the staff does this. In turn, the state directors give orders to area directors, and again, the state staff people give no orders. Area directors give orders to the operating units under their direction and in their area. Here, again, the area staff issues no orders.

Here, then, as our definition said, we have a chain of organization units (national, state, and area), operating under authority given them or delegated from the administrator; and at various points (national, state, and area) there are groups of people called staff, whose function or duty is advisory, as distinguished from the function of command.

We should observe at this point that the state directors, in order to operate successfully in their state, must have the authority. This authority is given to them by the administrator; that is, they are told that they have the authority to direct all the activities in their state. (Their people are also told this.) In turn, area directors must have the authority to direct work in their area. They get this by delegation from the state director. If either the state or area directors could not act until they asked permission "up the line," the work would proceed very slowly. Thus, for large organizations, relatively extensive delegations of authority may be needed if the line people are to operate at full efficiency. In a very real sense, the state director *acts for* the administrator in the state. The area directors do the same thing for the state directors in their part (area) of the state.

In this larger organization (50 states, some 150 areas, and about 1,800 operating units) the same general rules are in effect—and the same kinds of problems occur—as in our very simple organization. Staff people who start giving orders cause confusion. Coordination and communications require special attention to keep the organization operating smoothly and efficiently.

Principles of Organization

We are now in a position to consider some principles or ideas that have been widely used to set up and run line-staff organizations.[1] These principles, if followed, will usually foster maximum efficiency and economy, involve the least confusion, and make the organization relatively easy to control.

1. The reader is urged to review the book *It All Depends* by Harvey Sherman (University of Alabama Press, 1966). The author calls this "a pragmatic approach to organization," meaning "doing what works in a given situation." The ideas expressed and discussed are highly useful to the practicing supervisor.

Also, coordination can be achieved reasonably well. What we are saying is that if you have an organization based on the following principles, the people who compose it will find it easier, more efficient, and less expensive to operate. We should note before we start that no matter how well organized a business or an agency may be, it cannot function at peak efficiency *unless the people in it use it properly.* With this proviso in mind, we may review the principles of organization as follows:

1. *Lines of authority in the organization must be clear.*

The lines of authority, or chains of command, must be well known to everyone in the organization. In the larger organization outlined above we have already noted the line running from the administrator to the state director, to the area director, to the operating units. There are, however, some other lines of authority that must be noted. For example, if there is a director of the administrative staff with, say, three divisions, each divided into several sections, there would be lines of authority between the heads of these groupings. We can chart this as follows:

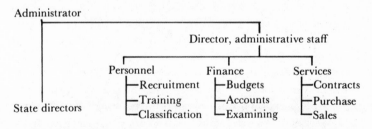

In this administrative staff group there is a line of authority from the director to the head of personnel, and thence to the sections on recruitment, training, and classification. There are similar lines through the finance division and the services division. You need not become confused on finding a "line" in a staff organization. The lines you see here are chains of command for just a segment of the total organization, that is, for the administrative staff group alone. This branch line does not conflict in any way with the main line from the administrator to the state directors, and on. The orders that flow over the branch line have largely to do with the administrative work of the various divisions.

As a corollary to our principle that lines of authority must be clear, it should also be noted that these channels of authority should not be violated by staff units. We have already seen the trouble that can develop even in a simple organization when staff people try to assume command. There is another problem of the same kind when a staff office in one location begins giving orders directly to a staff office in another place. For example, in the chart shown below, the orders having to do with personnel matters should go from the administrator to the state director.

Orders should *not* flow from the director of the administrator's personnel staff to the director of the state director's personnel staff, as shown here by the dotted line. Orders should not flow between staff units *unless* the administrator has delegated authority for such action and everyone concerned understands the situation. Generally speaking, an administrator may safely permit routine and procedural matters to flow directly over the dotted line between the two staff divisions. But it is throwing the baby away with the bath to permit personnel staff to direct most or all of the personnel work in the organization. This is a serious error, since personnel matters are of key importance in any organization and, hence, of primary concern to line officers.

2. *Everyone in the organization should know* (a) *to whom he or she reports,* (b) *who reports to him or her; and no one should report to more than one supervisor.*

This is the principle of organization that is often called the "unity-of-command" principle. Any person who must report to two or three bosses is in for trouble. What does that person do if he or she gets conflicting orders? Whose order does the person carry out? And which order does the person carry out first?

This principle of organization may seem so obvious and so necessary that little emphasis needs to be placed on it. Even so, it is frequently violated, sometimes carelessly, sometimes unconsciously, by the very people who claim it to be obvious. We have already noted in our first principle of supervision that everyone should know who the supervisor is and that there should be only one. Sometimes organization charts show what the correct situation should be, but in actual fact some people may have two supervisors and others none at all. A weak person in a supervisory job may sometimes let a stronger person in the group of people assume command. All this makes for confusion, inefficiency, and of course, poor morale.

3. *The responsibility and authority of each supervisor should be understood by everyone concerned.*

This principle applies, you will note, both to the supervisors and to the people they supervise. Everyone must understand in order that everyone can operate properly. The responsibility and authority are best expressed in writing, which is a fairly universal practice in the federal government but less so in industry. This helps to make the matter clear; but here again, activity in careless disregard of the principle can defeat even a clearly stated job description.

Let us note also that no individual or unit of an organization can be held responsible for the successful performance of any job unless the responsibility carries with it the authority to complete the job. Responsibility and authority must go hand in hand (see Principle 5, below).

4. *The number of people reporting to one supervisor should be no more than the number whose efforts he or she can effectively direct and coordinate.*

This is often called the principle of span of control. The idea is that if the span is too wide, the supervisor cannot give proper attention to each person. To understand the implications of this idea, we must classify supervisors into two kinds: (a) those who supervise other supervisors, whom we shall call managers, and (b) those who supervise workers on a job, whom we shall call first-line supervisors.

The number of workers first-line supervisors can have reporting to them depends on a great many things. They may be doing some work themselves other than supervision; in this case the number of people they can supervise depends in part on how much other work they are expected to do. This is a common enough situation in many organizations, but one we will not treat here, since it is a job mixture that has to be treated as an individual situation.

First-line supervisors who do nothing but supervise, ordinarily have from ten to twenty people reporting to them. The number depends on whether the group is all in one place or separated geographically. It depends also on how many new problems come up from day to day, and on how closely the work of one person interlocks with that of another. Where the people work together in one place, where all the people know quite well how to deal with the daily problems, and where there is very little overlapping of jobs, the supervisor can supervise the largest number of people. The more spread out the work is, or the closer the jobs interlock, or the more frequently new problems arise, the fewer people the supervisor can direct.

With respect to managers who supervise other supervisors,

the situation is somewhat different. Even here, geographic spread, interlocking work, and new problems affect the number of supervisors that can report to one manager. But in addition, the work is entirely mental and may possibly demand more of a supervisor. As a matter of fact, there has been a great deal of argument about how many supervisors or executives one manager can direct. Many textbooks will tell you that the limit is five and will refer you to the work of a man named Graicunas who "proved" this mathematically.[2] There seems nothing wrong with Graicunas' mathematics, but there are many who disagree with the assumptions on which it is based. Other books will tell you that the idea of five is nonsense, and that there are plenty of well-managed corporations where the spans of control for managers run up to twenty-four or more.[3]

We may note here that the span of control in the government varies widely—as it does in business and industry. In some agencies four or five people commonly report to one manager; in others, as many as fifty report to one executive. In both situations the agencies may be well managed and successful. We can say, however, that an agency as well as a company is wise to study carefully the many factors affecting the span of control for its managers. The real question is: How does it work? The span should not be so wide that coordination and direction deteriorate, nor so narrow that the manager is literally "breathing down the necks" of the people. Careful testing and evaluation of results may have to be conducted over a long period to be sure the spans used are reasonably correct for each organizational situation.

5. *Authority to act should be delegated insofar as possible to the units or individuals nearest the point where the action must take place.*

Supervisors on the firing line usually know better than

2. See Lyndall F. Urwick, "The Manager's Span of Control," *Harvard Business Review,* May–June 1956, for a complete discussion of this.

3. This is discussed by W. W. Suojanen in "The Span of Control—Fact or Fable?", *Advanced Management,* November 1955.

anyone else what the problems are and what must be done to overcome them. They have the best grasp of the conditions surrounding their work. They know the people involved, they see the need for action, and they urgently need to take the action called for by the situation. To make them check "up the line" every time they want to do something not only wastes their time but also wastes the time of the people up the line. They should not have to decide on every detail of action in every supervised unit.

Supervisors need authority to decide what to do and to act in the area of activity they are capable of judging locally. This authority should be delegated to them, and they should be held responsible for using it properly. To begin with, of course, the supervisors selected should have the ability to use necessary authority wisely.

6. *Every function needed to accomplish the organization's purpose should be assigned to a unit of the organization.*

It seems obvious that all the jobs to be done should be assigned to one unit or another of the organization. It is not unusual to find, however, that some particular job has been left hanging in the air and that confusion results when several units try to take care of it at the same time. Here we need again to note that functions assigned to units should be clear, specific, and easily understood. It goes almost without saying that all this should be in writing. This is one of the reasons for organization charts.

7. *The organization should be as simple as possible.*

The idea applies especially to the number of so-called levels. For example, in the following chart, organization B appears simpler than organization A.

In this example, working in organization A will generally be more difficult than in B. Orders from the national director will take longer to reach the sixth level in the county than in B where it is the third level. Information will take longer to go either up or down the line, and there are more places where the orders may be "interpreted," that is, changed. In A county directors, tired of waiting for urgently needed decisions, may make an "end run"—that is, if they can get away with it, they will try to reach the regional or the national director without going through all the directors in between. This by-passing of levels will cause confusion, and there are many examples of it to be found in organizations with too many levels. We cannot put all the blame for the end runs on county directors; a simpler organization would remove the temptation and the necessity.

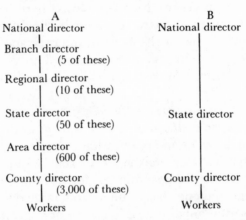

A	B
National director	National director
Branch director (5 of these)	
Regional director (10 of these)	
State director (50 of these)	State director
Area director (600 of these)	
County director (3,000 of these)	County director
Workers	Workers

We must note that while organization B is simpler with respects to levels, the directors in it necessarily have a much wider span of control than those in A. In A the span of control for any director is 5, except for the state director, who has 12. In B the span of control is 50 for the national director and 50 to 100 or more for the state director. A simple device for cutting down these latter spans, which are too wide, is to divide very large states into two or three areas, each with a director. Smaller states need not be so divided. This introduces an additional level in organization B, but only to a limited extent, and only for special situations.

There are many ways in which organizations can get too

complex. Too many small staff units at each level, instead of a few combined, larger ones, can slow down staff operation. Too many assistants, each with a small segment of work to watch over, can slow down the work. Mixed-up staff units at different levels can cause trouble; for example, if payrolls are prepared by a financial staff at one level but by a personnel staff at another level, then coordination becomes more difficult.

All such examples—and there are many more—lead us to the need for constant review of any organization structure. Just because an organization has always been organized in a particular way is no reason why it should keep on in the same way indefinitely. Both in industry and in government, "organizational paralysis" has led to disaster often enough. The need for change leads us finally to our last principle.

8. *An organization should be flexible, but ordinarily changes in it should be made gradually except under highly special conditions.*

It is one thing for an organization to be flexible, but quite another for it to be shaken or rocked by administrative earthquakes. In the government, for example, possibly as much waste of money has resulted from large-scale reorganizations as from any other action. New administrators, especially those of limited experience, are often prone to move too quickly in reorganizing an agency. Instead of studying their agency carefully, then changing the organization structure gradually, they move on the basis of preconception to bring about a good "shake-up." The moment word gets out—which it does with great speed regardless (or even because) of secrecy—the wildest rumors streak through the agency. People gather in small groups to speculate about the impending changes. Work, except routine stuff, comes almost to a standstill. Many people leave for jobs elsewhere. The rest wait to see what is going to happen—a very natural reaction to any kind of impending change. The deterioration of a formerly smoothly operating agency and the consequent loss in productive output are tremendous and unnecessary.

In contrast, experienced administrators work with the people on their staff and, indeed, with their whole organization, on the new objectives that should be reached. Once these are clear, they begin making small moves to reform their organization, so that it can most easily reach these objectives. Reorganization goes on all the time, but always aimed at objectives the whole organization understands. Implicit in this more gradual approach is the realization that organizations are made up of *people,* and that trained, experienced people are the greatest asset an organization has. It is not change that hurts an organization but rather failure on the part of the leaders of an organization to supply its people with timely information about the change.

Some Ideas on Staff Work

Before we leave our consideration of organization, it may be worthwhile to add a final note on the operation of staff people. Somehow, in many organizations, staff personnel begin to feel they are not really playing a proper part in the program going on. Their advice may not be taken; they may not even be asked for it. Administrators may make decisions without reference to their staff specialists; indeed, they may become impatient with the kind of staff advice they receive. Sometimes this failure results in quite serious consequences. And there may be a great many reasons why staff and line people are unable to work together.

Some years ago an idea was widely circulated in the Department of Defense and, since then, elsewhere in the government service. The idea seems to have come originally from an official paper by Major General Archer L. Learch. It had to do with what is called completed staff work. The suggestions apply both to the line officer and to the staff officer. They are shown in the chart on the following page.

COMPLETED STAFF WORK

How to Get It	How to Do It
Assign the problem and request its solution in such a way that completed staff work is readily possible.	Study the problem and present its solution in such form that only approval or disapproval of the completed action is required.
1. Know the problem.	1. Work out all details completely.
2. Make one individual responsible to you for the solution.	2. Consult other staff officers.
3. State the problem to him clearly, precisely; explain reasons, background; limit the area to be studied.	3. Study, write; restudy, rewrite.
4. Give the individual the advantage of your knowledge and experience in this problem.	4. Present a single, coordinated, proposed action. Do not equivocate.
5. Set a time limit; or request assignee to estimate completion date.	5. Do not present long memoranda or explanations. Correct solutions are usually recognizable.
6. Assure him that you are available for discussion as work progresses.	6. Advise the chief what to do. Do not ask him.
If you were the subordinate, would *you* consider the guidance, given at the time the assignment is made and as the directed work progresses, to be adequate for readily completed staff work? Adequate guidance eliminates wasted effort and makes for completed staff work.	If you were the chief, would *you* sign the paper you have prepared and thus stake your professional reputation on its being right? If not, take it back and work it over, it is not yet completed staff work. —*From the U.S. Department of Defense*

Some Conclusions

We are now in a position to state a few general conclusions about organizations that supervisors may want to keep in mind, as follows:

1. While all supervisors scarcely need to be experts on organization theory, they do need to be fully familiar with the organization of which they and their people are a part. They ought to be able to draw a chart of their agency, showing its line and staff units and what each does and is responsible for. Obviously, they should know who the people are who handle the various units of their outfit, most especially those who may deal fairly closely with the work of their group.

2. Every supervisor should be familiar with the principles of organization, such as those we have discussed in this chapter. These principles may be stated in different ways, but the ideas they express have stood up pretty well for many centuries. Almost certainly, better principles will be found as we learn more about how to work together. In the meantime, it behooves supervisors to know the best there is to know, so that they may contribute intelligently to the improvement of their own organization. It is possible that some supervisors will be called upon sooner or later to help reorganize or to set up an agency or a unit of one. It would be well if they were prepared.

3. Obviously, organization structure is important only in relation to the people composing it. Supervisors should remember that no organization, no matter how perfect, can survive and succeed unless the people within it work together for its survival and success.

4. The people in an organization must never lose sight of the objective or purpose of their organization. In a large, far-flung organization this is not always an easy thing to do, but its objective is the key to all the work it does.

5. Communications within an organization must always

be kept in top operating condition. Any time the people come to feel that they do not know and understand what is going on, the work of the organization is in danger of falling off. If the communications become bad enough, an organization may eventually segment itself into a mass of fragments subsisting largely on the grapevine.

6. What may be called the "administrative climate" of an organization must be a good one. The management and supervisory people are the ones who generate the climate. It should be one in which people are not afraid to speak their mind or be fearful of reprisals if they indulge in some original thinking. It should be such that people enjoy working in it, enjoy their work, and take pride in their organization. The idea applies equally to the organization as a whole and to each small supervisory unit within it.[4]

7. And finally, in summary, it is of key importance that managers and supervisors of the organization understand that the most valuable asset is its people. It is never in the interest of good administration to sacrifice people to organizational changes or arrangements. No organizational theory can long survive that is in conflict with sound principles of human behavior and human relations.[5]

4. See also Likert's "System 4" type of organization, described on page 108.
5. To understand fully all that may be involved in items 3, 6, and 7 above, the serious student may find it useful to study *Integrating the Individual and the Organization* by Chris Argyris (New York: Wiley, 1964).

13

About Supervisors*

We are now in a position to develop a summary of sorts about supervisors. To start, we must point out what a supervisor ought to be doing, based on the best available evidence:

1. A supervisor's chief role is to help a team of people to get their work done. The supervisor is most emphatically *not* there to direct, control, or regulate the manner in which the work is to be done, the exact steps each person should take, and the specific way in which the work should be carried on.

This is a difficult point to get across. The supervisor is a leader, right? Then who's to direct, control, and regulate the action if not the supervisor? The answer is *the group of people working* at a job, including, but not limited to, the supervisor. All our most successful research points to this conclusion [4, 6, 7]. The success of Lincoln Electric of Cleveland[5] and of numerous industrial organizations in Japan and elsewhere[8, 9, 10, 11, 12], as operated with American workers in our country, and changes undertaken in this direction by a number of major American industries[4, 8] all point to the same conclusion, i.e., *teamwork.*

Lincoln makes an interesting point about this matter. He notes [5 p. 150] that to develop a team that can win in the

* Numbers in brackets refer to the list of references at the end of this chapter.

world's competitive markets, to say nothing of our own markets in this country, a supervisor or manager "must care for the well-being and development of every man in the plant *just as an athletic coach looks out for every member of his team.*"

2. As a corollary to the first point, a supervisor should avoid becoming a bottleneck. Many supervisors in American organizations unfortunately are simply exactly that. Their failures and mistakes block the otherwise high productivity of their organizations. This is especially true of highly placed supervisors—often called managers—who have been taught how to become effective bottlenecks, unfortunately, on their way up the career ladder.

Worth repeating here is a little anecdote about this matter of bottlenecks. It seems that the admiral of the fleet was holding a special conference on the flagship in the South Pacific. The group was considering a serious bottleneck that had developed and that was preventing the great fleet from becoming effective. There seemed to be no solution. Then one officer spoke up. "Why don't we get a sailor off this ship, sir," he said, addressing the admiral. "Maybe," the officer went on, "maybe the fighting man on the ship will have an idea about this bottleneck and how to cure it."

The admiral nodded sagely. "You may have something there," he said, then turning to his aide—"bring in the first sailor you meet when you go out the door." In short order a young sailor appeared, saluted promptly, and stood at attention.

"Son," said the admiral kindly, "Son, what do you know about bottlenecks?" The group leaned forward, all attention.

"Sir," the young sailor said, "Sir, I believe they usually occur at the *top* of the bottle!"

Now, how many clogged bottlenecks do we have in the United States, in business, industry, government, labor unions, educational systems, religious institutions, and every other kind of organization we use? The answer is: enough to keep America from occupying first place in world production as it used to do [1, 7, 10].

3. It is obvious that the full effectiveness of an ideal supervisor will take place only as he or she fully trusts his or her people, and as the team of people trust the supervisor. True cooperation depends on trust, and since cooperative effort is essential to the highest productivity, it is a wise and skillful supervisor who spares no pains to develop it. This effort in turn depends on how well the supervisor understands what motivates people [2, 3].

Despite current thought to the contrary, the motivation of people at work is not solely the amount of money they can earn. True, the services of people are paid for in money, and the greater the service, the more money is earned—at least theoretically. But people work for far more than money. They work because they love their tasks. They work to show how good they are. They work in order to be of greater service to clients or customers. In fact, people work for a great many reasons not necessarily related to money at all.

(Why do you suppose a friend of mine was able to write me recently that the line of people trying to get a job at Lincoln Electric in Cleveland was something on the order of five miles long? See pp. 68–71 of this book for your answer.)

One of the reasons people quit jobs is because the possibility of ego satisfaction, i.e., motivation, is not present.

4. A skillful supervisor needs the full-fledged help of the team of supervised people. How this is organized varies considerably with the kind of work, the skills of the people involved, and so on. But policies, plans, innovations in the work need the attention not only of the supervisor but of the entire team. It helps enormously if the people on the team are proud of their product and of the organization for which they work [4]. This is all the more reason for good work, both in quality and quantity—a point that any worker can see as well as a supervisor.

There is an idea well known to the psychologists—the self-fulfilling prophecy we have already talked about: what people are told they may become, they do indeed try to become; and in the trying, they often succeed. Parents tell their children that they will do great things in the world, and they do. Or parents tell their children that they're dumb—and so they become so. All this may only irritate some; others may have experienced a self-fulfilling prophecy and will nod and smile with understanding. (See Chapter 3 for a full discussion of this.) Thus, in the supervisor–supervised situation, the supervisor can frequently—even though not always—succeed in getting his or her people to do great things because the people come to believe that they can, and they do.

In J. Sterling Livingston's article in the *Harvard Business Review* for July–August 1969, he sets forth several general criteria affecting managerial success resulting from his and other work:

> What a manager expects of his subordinates and the way he treats them largely determine their performance and career success.
>
> A unique characteristic of superior managers is their ability to create high performance expectations that subordinates fulfill.
>
> Less effective managers fail to develop similar expectations and as a consequence, the productivity of their subordinates suffers.
>
> Subordinates, more often than not, appear to do what they believe they are expected to do.

5. We come now to some things to avoid. These have to do with attitudes largely as expressed in action and language [1]. Most of this has to do with the attitudes of what are generally known as "superiors" toward the "inferiors" who do the work. This attitude varies all the way from downright contempt to an almost unconscious downgrading.

But even the organization charts we draw have top management and subordinate groupings. When such charts are drawn in Japan, they are not drawn vertically; they look much like our flowcharts, reading from left to right—if they are drawn at all. Of course, because a man or woman is working with a supervisor does not mean that the person has automatically become inferior in some way.

(We could proceed to summarize more things a supervisor ought to do, but they require some special steps, so we consider them in the concluding chapters of this book.)

The superior versus other designations have even less validity in our new participative ideal of working. Participative management [4] is applicable worldwide, anywhere on the planet where human beings work, in organizations of infinite variety. The participative system, to quote Likert, is "applicable to every kind of organization . . . throughout the world." Two things are needed: (1) an appropriate structure in the organization designed to provide for the participation to work, and (2) effective participation of the humans involved. There is no use urging participation if the people in command of the organization really do not intend for it to work.

A number of organizations have adopted all or parts of the Japanese type of management, which is generally participative in nature; the list includes Motorola, Ford, several branches of General Motors, including especially Buick, and a number of government agencies. Unfortunately, some have adopted the quality circle (QC) idea only. This involves getting a group of workers together, at intervals, to consider ways and means of improving the quality and quantity of work. The QC operation works for a while and then frequently dies. The principal trouble is that the QCs are only a part of a system. Unless top management institutes the whole system of participative management, the QCs cannot successfully continue.

What stands in the way of a fully participative work force? Usually the person in charge—the very person who should accept people's ideas and assistance. Indeed, in all the teaching I have done, all the discussions held, all the projects assisted, one persistent fact stands clear. This fact is the belief by these supervisors that while they agreed fully, with few or no reservations, with the ideas discussed in their group, they felt helpless about getting the boss to accept the ideas.

Most supervisors of the present day have been trained by *their* supervisors in how to supervise. And the training—conscious or unconscious—has been largely of the authoritative type [4]. Thus it seems clear that the operating heads of organizations must be converted to the participative type of management before the managers and supervisors of their organization will begin to change. James Lincoln was successful because he began participative management from his first act as head of Lincoln Electric.

To learn more about these ideas and their successful practice, I recommend that the supervisor study the following books. If the supervisor is really interested in becoming "one of the best," then here is a good place to start.

Literature Cited*

1. *The Competitive Status of the U.S. Auto Industry.* Washington, D.C.: National Academy of Engineering of the National Academy of Sciences, 1982. 203 pages.
2. Herzberg, Frederick, *The Managerial Choice.* Homewood, Ill.: Irwin, 1976. 360 pages.
3. Izard, Carroll E., *Human Emotions.* New York: Plenum, 1977. 495 pages.
4. Likert, Rensis, and Jane Gibson Likert, *New Ways of Managing Conflict.* New York: McGraw-Hill, 1976. 373 pages.
5. Lincoln, James F., *A New Approach to Industrial Economics.* New York: Devin-Adair, 1961. 165 pages.
6. McGregor, Douglas, *The Human Side of Enterprise.* New York: McGraw-Hill, 1960. 246 pages.

* Although most of these books are listed in Chapter 16, those pertaining to participative management are listed here for ease of reference.

7. Marrow, Alfred J., David E. Bowers, and Stanley E. Seashore, *Management By Participation*. New York: Harper & Row, 1967. 264 pages.
8. Ouchi, William, *Theory Z*. Reading, Mass.: Addison-Wesley, 1981. 283 pages.
9. Pascale, R. T., and Anthony G. Athos, *The Art of Japanese Management*. New York: Simon & Schuster, 1981, New York: Warner, 1982.
10. Sagan, Carl, *The Dragons of Eden*. New York: Random House, 1977. 271 pages.
11. Servan-Schreiber, Jean-Jaques, *The World Challenge*. New York: Simon & Schuster, 1980. 302 pages.
12. Vogel, Ezra F., *Japan as Number One*. Cambridge, Mass.: Harvard University Press, 1979. 272 pages.

14

Some Management Activities

So far, we have been giving most of our attention to the ways in which supervisors and their people can work together. We have done this because every supervisor is concerned with ideas such as these. But other kinds of activities are also essential to the work of a unit of organization. These are different in character from the strictly human relations, and they have much to do with the way in which the unit functions. For our purposes we may call them management activities, although we must note that "management" is a word of many meanings. (Sometimes management is used to mean both supervision and the direction of operating systems. It is also used to denote the directing group of an organization. This group is often called "top management" or simply "management.")

Management, as we use the word here, depends on the size and kind of organization segment headed by a supervisor. All supervisors must perform some of these management activities, but some supervisors deal with more than others. For example, every supervisor must plan and schedule work, but not every supervisor must develop financial plans (that is, budgets), since not all supervisors are concerned with the management of funds. Similarly, not all supervisors manage communication systems, although every supervisor must be skilled in communicating with the people in the unit.

In this chapter we consider some ideas about work loads, planning, scheduling, and the efficiency with which work is done. Such things as these are matters concerning every supervisor, not just a few in top management.

Work Loads

The amount of work supervisors and their people must do each day, or week, or month, or year is commonly spoken of as their work load. This is something in which all of us are considerably interested. Usually the work load varies in some way from period to period, alternately reaching high and low points, depending on the kind of work being done. Supervisors have to make whatever advance arrangements they can to be sure their people are not overloaded part of the time and only partly occupied the rest of the time. More than this, the load must be fairly shared by all the people in the unit. No one should have to carry more—or less—than a fair share, and importantly also, the various kinds of work should be correctly assigned to the proper people. This helps to avoid using high-priced people to do low-priced work, or the reverse.

In any event, there is a simple way to study or review work loads in relation to people that will help a supervisor considerably in dealing with these problems. The method is often called work-load analysis. We make such an analysis to find out:

1. What the various jobs are that make up the work load.
2. How many jobs of each kind there are to do.
3. About how long it will take to do each kind of job.
4. Who can best do each kind of job, in terms of kinds and grades or salaries of personnel.

Once we have the facts about each one of these four items clearly set forth, we are in a position to judge whether our unit is correctly staffed, whether the work is correctly assigned and shared, and what steps might be necessary to correct any unbalanced situation that may come to light.

The first thing we have to do is to state as precisely as we can what the work load is for a given period of time. For certain kinds of work we might do this on a daily basis. For example, in a janitor job, there may be a hundred rooms and forty thousand square feet of hallways to be cleaned each night. Or for a typist pool, there may be an average of three hundred pages a day to be typed. However, we would not use a daily rate for a group of lawyers who might be expected to prepare two hundred briefs each year. Thus a supervisor must select for review a period of time that has most meaning for the particular kind of work. These periods are affected by all sorts of conditions, such as climate (for agricultural workers), pay periods (for payroll units), weather (for janitor groups), congressional sessions (for budget groups), court sessions (for lawyers), and so on.

We might note, in passing, some symptoms that may indicate the need for a work-load study. An obvious one is the apparent need for continuous overtime work. Another is a backlog of some kind that never seems to get done. Another is that Joe always seems to have more than he can do while Susie never seems to keep busy. Still another is that no one ever seems to make use of some of the work turned out, and there is doubt about whether it really needs to keep on being done. And so on. Usually it is not enough to try to deal directly with such symptoms. They indicate that something is out of adjustment; the question is, what?

Almost always, as we go ahead to make a work-load analysis, we find that the total load of work is made up of a group or series of jobs. For example, in the janitor job mentioned above, the force may actually have to do a variety of things, such as:

Sweep 100 rooms.
Wash 40,000 square feet of hallways.
Vacuum-clean 40 rugs.

Empty 120 wastebaskets.
Dust desks, tables, chairs, and files in 100 rooms.
Collect soap, brooms, cleaners, and other supplies from supply room and haul to area. Return these at end of job.

This breakdown into a series of jobs is usually possible for all but the simplest work loads. Such a breakdown should consist of jobs or groups of jobs that are performed more or less as units. We do this in order to be able to say about how long each unit ought to take. In our janitor example, experience may have shown that it takes about 12 minutes to sweep a room, about 20 minutes to vacuum a rug, and so on. On such a basis, we can then say that it will require 1,200 minutes, or 20 hours, to sweep 100 rooms, and 800 minutes, or 13 hours, to vacuum 40 rugs. All these data begin to get a little cumbersome itemized this way, so we organize them on a simple sheet like this:

Kind of Job	Number	Rate	TOTAL TIME REQUIRED (hours)
Sweep rooms	100	12 min	1,200 min = 20
Vacuum rugs	40	20 min	800 min = 13
Dust furniture in rooms	100	15 min	1,500 min = 25
Wash hallway floors (sq ft)	40,000	1 hr/ 1,000 sq ft	= 40
Empty wastebaskets	120	5 min	600 min = 10

As we list the kinds of jobs, their number, and the rate at which each one can be done, we are then able to see the time needed to take care of each part of the work load and, finally, the total time required for all of it.

This analysis still does not tell us what kinds of people should be doing each job. Let us suppose, for the sake of example, that we can use grade-one people to dust, sweep, and empty wastebaskets, but that we need grade-three people to handle the machines used for vacuuming rugs and washing floors. Our analysis form will need a little expansion as shown below.

Kind of Job	Number	Rate	TIME REQUIRED (hours)		
			Grade 1	Grade 3	Total
Sweep rooms	100	12 min	20		20
Vacuum rugs	40	20 min		13	13
Dust furniture in rooms	100	15 min	25		25
Wash hallway floors sq ft	40,000	1 hr 1,000 sq ft		40	40
Empty wastebaskets	120	5 min	10		10
Total			55	53	108

Thus far our analysis seems to show the need for about seven people in grade one and very close to seven in grade three. (We get this by dividing the totals by eight hours.) But this is not all there is to it. There are a number of incidental jobs that are sure to come up—something spilled on a rug takes special cleaning; a cracked desk glass needs reporting; a number of light bulbs need changing, etc. All these, if handled by the same force, take time too and must be allowed for on some kind of basis.

Last, note that if there is need for 108 hours of work per night, then this cannot be done by 14 people unless this is *all* they do. Coffee breaks, special jobs, staff meetings, sick and annual leave, and the like take time and must be counted. Also, of course, someone is needed to supervise the entire operation. That person's work does not include sweeping, dusting, and other such services, but rather checking, training, guiding, evaluating production, making work-load studies, and the like—that is, *supervising*.

In making a work-load analysis, a supervisor will do well to keep such points as the following in mind:

1. The list of jobs to be done should not be too detailed. If the work is broken into a long series of very small parts, the analysis is likely to become bogged down in the mass of details. In our janitor example, we could have shown the exact number of chairs, large tables, small tables, file cases, telephone stands, etc., necessary to be dusted, with a rate for each one. But from a practical standpoint, a supervisor can afford to group them all into one item of "furniture per room," since he or she knows pretty well what each room will contain. The point here is that we make a work-load analysis to help us get a job done, not just for the sake of an elaborate study itself. Being too elaborate about such a study is characteristic of inexperienced supervisors.

2. The rates, that is, the average time per job unit, have to be set with reasonable accuracy. There are a number of ways of finding out what they are. One is to check a number of people as they work to find out what a good average rate is. Another is to divide the total time it takes to do a large number of such jobs by the number completed. Results from these two methods can be compared to see how well they coincide.

The impulse is often almost overwhelming to cut the rates down. It may appear that if everyone worked just a little harder, considerably more work could be accomplished. But the catch is in whether everyone is going to "work a little harder." Here, a supervisor will do well to remember the difference between a driver and a leader, and to recollect that participation of the people in making such analyses may often provide many new ways of dealing with the situation. People who are proud of their outfit will be quite ingenious in suggesting ways to improve rates—and in carrying them out. People who are resentful at being handed rates they disagree with are quite unlikely to reach them, except under heavy prodding, with consequent ill feeling and with slow-downs the moment pressure is relaxed.

3. Distributing work among various kinds and grades of personnel requires a supervisor to know a little about job classification. In our janitor example, the distinction is between only two kinds, but a great many kinds may be required for more complex work. In the engineering work of the government service, for example, there are nine grades of engineering technicians. In what grade of work is each job? Or in many kinds of professional work, as many as eighteen grades may be available to choose from.

Note that we cannot afford to select the grade and kind of personnel simply on the basis of what has always been done before. This needs rechecking and reevaluating from time to time, especially because either the work or the classification standards may change. If we are wrong in our classification of personnel and grades, our whole analysis becomes far less useful.

Drawing Conclusions

Once we have completed a work-load analysis, and are satisfied that the picture it portrays is reasonably accurate, we begin to consider what we need to do about the findings. Three general items may show up:

1. We may find that we have the wrong kinds of people doing certain jobs. This may seem a little silly, but it is quite common. It often occurs that skilled people devote part or most of their time to unskilled work. Since skilled people command higher pay, the work then costs more than it should. If unskilled people are performing a lot of skilled work, either their work is not as good as it should be; or there is doubt whether the work really calls for skill; or the unskilled people possibly have become skilled and should be reclassified.

It is common enough also to find people doing the wrong

kind of work in areas where a distinction is made between professional and subprofessional work. What kind of work is professional? How much subprofessional work should a professional person do? The two kinds of work are often very closely associated and hard to separate. Ambitious subprofessional people may often try to do more of the professional work than they possibly should. What guides do we use here?

It is well to keep in mind that professional and skilled workers are more highly paid than are subprofessional or unskilled. Thus people who are professional or skilled will cost more, and their efforts should be directed to the kind of work for which they are best fitted. It is also well for government supervisors to keep in mind precisely stated classification standards and specifications for jobs in the government service. These—with the help of a classification analyst—can be of real use to a supervisor faced with problems of this kind.

2. We may find that some of our people are in the wrong grade, that is, they are being paid either too much or too little for the kind of work they are doing. Either situation presents a problem that should be dealt with promptly, since either situation means an injustice is being done to someone. Because position grades must be set with due regard for classification standards and specifications, here again the supervisor may wish to consult a classification specialist for help.

3. We may find that we have too many, or too few, people in total, or that we have too many of one kind of personnel and too few of another. In any case, the supervisor must plan on making such adjustments as seem called for. In this case, one's own supervisor should be consulted and, in the end, the personnel office.

4. We may find—or know already—that the work load fluctuates, hitting a high point, every so often, that the regular working group simply cannot handle. There are two ways to deal with this:

a.   We may ask members of the unit to work overtime for short periods in order to meet the deadlines involved.

b.   We may employ additional people on a temporary basis to help tide over the high period.

Planning and Scheduling

Supervisors cannot do much of a job unless they have clearly in mind what they intend to do the next day, next week, next month, and next year. Some kinds of work call for looking farther ahead than others. But every kind requires that careful thought be given to what should be done in the future. The business of deciding ahead of time what we will do when the time comes is generally spoken of as planning. A good supervisor must, without question, also be a good planner.

A plan of work can be set up conveniently for about a year ahead. This is not too long a time to be impractical, nor so short as to keep us constantly developing new plans. For some supervisors, two, three, or five years may be better. Others may want to plan no more than a few months ahead. And indeed, there are no rules for this. One uses the period of time best suited to the work being done. But whatever period is chosen, a simple way to proceed is as follows:

1. We look ahead over the period and think of the important jobs we hope to get done. As we do this, we consider the resources we have, in human resources, materials, supplies, equipment, and other items. We write down all the things we hope to accomplish in a simple list. To start with, we do not have to worry about which comes first; we can arrange the items later. And we write until we cannot think of any more subjects; if we find that we have omitted some, we add them. It is not necessary to describe each item in detail: each one should be explicit enough to call to mind what is intended.

2. The items are rearranged in some sort of order. Most

supervisors find that they cannot accomplish everything they would like to in a single year—especially in view of available resources and staff. So first things are put first. Items on the tail end of the list may not get done—or they may, if everything works out as the supervisor hopes.

3. Next, the items can be expanded a little, with important details added and special phases given special attention.

4. Following this, something must be put down indicating *how* the job can best be done.

5. Next we can show *who* is going to do each job, that is, which people or person will be assigned to which item.

6. Finally, we begin to set some sort of timetable for getting things done. This leads us into *scheduling*.

It is obvious that material such as the foregoing may conveniently be arranged in some uniform manner, for example, on a columnar pad with headings something like these:

Job or Activity	How	Who	When Where (if necessary)
A numbered list of the things we plan on doing	Here we set forth the way we will do the things we plan	The people assigned to each job or activity	In these columns we can indicate when and where the work is to be done

Another useful format might be this:

Job	January	February	March	April	etc.
1.	In these columns Who, How, and Where				
2.	are listed for each item.				
3.					

The list and format above are merely suggestive. There are all sorts of ways to develop a plan and to put it in usable form. All of them must rely on a clear conception on the part of the planner. No format or written list has any greater value than the thinking one does about the future needs and work.

Scheduling

Some supervisors prefer to combine their timetable with their plans. Others prefer to develop a plan that contains only deadline dates for completion of an item or only general indications of the period when the work will be performed. Whether timetables or schedules are prepared as part of a plan or separately, however, *they had better be prepared.* Various studies have shown that there is a high degree of correlation between good scheduling and high productivity. Putting this another way, well-scheduled work is likely to get done in a more orderly way and at less cost.

Some ideas about scheduling that have proved valuable are these:

1. If you try to make only a single schedule for a long period ahead, you may discover that it is impossible to be precise about things many months ahead. For this reason it may be better to develop two kinds of schedules rather than only one. The first is a long-term schedule, say for a full year ahead. In this schedule the timing is somewhat general in character, as for example, "spring," "fall," "late August," and the like. Specific dates are put in the long-term schedule only when they are certainly known far ahead of time.

The second schedule is a short-term one, used to cover a period from one to several weeks ahead. Actually this is the immediate portion of a long-term schedule crystallized for specific action. In this one we can get specific not only on days but also on the time of day, if we like.

2. Schedules should be developed steadily. As the year rolls along, you can add items and general dates on the far

end of the long-term schedule, while the nearer portions are eaten up by the short-term schedule. The short-term schedule must be prepared at short intervals of a week or two, or ahead of whatever other interval you may be using.

3. Schedule everything to be done, insofar as practical. Obviously, despite the most careful scheduling, unexpected matters will come up that will strain or break your schedule. Even so, this is not a valid reason for neglecting to schedule all jobs and activities. The more fully you can organize your work into a schedule, the nearer you can come to peak efficiency.

4. Hold to your schedule as closely as practical. It is, of course, foolish to adhere blindly to a schedule simply because it has been set. You should run the schedule; do not let it run you. But again, the closer you can come to your schedule, the better for your work. Never deviate from it without good reason.

5. Plan for the unexpected. Since everyone knows that unexpected matters will come up from time to time, it is wise to provide for them in your schedule. At judicious intervals your schedule ought to have openings in it for the nonscheduled matters. This allows for emergency adjustment. It is another way of saying that too tight a schedule often comes to grief.

6. Coordinate your schedule with those of people who work with you. It is obviously preferable to do this ahead of time rather than be forced to change your timetable on short notice.

7. Keep your schedule showing. It is very important that the people with whom you work know that you have a schedule and that you stick to it rather closely. People cannot respect your schedule if they do not know you have one. Posting a schedule on the wall or bulletin board is generally a good thing to do in any office. Review it frequently.

8. Analyze completed schedules from time to time to see if

you could have prepared a better one in the light of the way things finally worked out. You may discover that you have a habit of scheduling too tightly or too loosely, of omitting things, of abandoning your schedule when you should have stuck to it, etc. A critical review of finished schedules will often provide you with ideas for making better ones. Experience is indeed a great teacher, if you use it.

Besides these suggested ideas, it is worth noting that schedules cannot plan and organize work. Their value is in setting forth plans on a time basis; usefulness in this respect is no greater than the excellence of the planning that must precede its use. Furthermore, supervisors who let their schedule control them instead of their controlling it are in for trouble. A schedule must be as flexible as possible. A rigid one can easily destroy the value of the planning.

Making Work-Improvement Studies

Anyone trying to do a job usually finds it can best get done in a number of steps. A little job may take only a few steps. A big job may take many. The series of steps to get the job done is usually called a procedure. Obviously, a short procedure containing a few steps is preferable to a long one containing many—provided the short procedure gets the job done just as well.

Job procedures may be called job methods or techniques, but by whatever name they are known, there is a tendency for them to grow. When many people are involved in the doing of a job, and everyone tries to get in on the act, it is inevitable that more steps begin to creep into the procedure used for getting it done.

Procedures are what they are not only because there are jobs to be done, but also because there is:

1. A law.
2. A regulation.
3. A policy.

In addition, there are other factors affecting procedures, including:

4. Custom.

5. Work habits.

6. Misunderstanding of policy (i.e., our "interpretation").

All these things can so modify a procedure as to change it from a simple set of steps to a complex grouping of many steps. All six factors tend to make a procedure longer. Worse, they tend to stifle initiative, stultify good judgment, increase costs, lengthen the time it takes to get the job done, and make work much harder than it need be.

When a procedure gets cumbersome enough, we say that it is "all fouled up in red tape." What we usually mean when we say this is that rules and regulations make it virtually impossible to operate without exasperating delay and a great many procedural steps. We do not usually mean that *we* cause the red tape, that is, that *our* work habits, or *our* customs, or *our* misunderstanding of policy, is creating the red tape.

The fact is, however, that any one or all of the six factors may operate to lengthen or complicate our procedures. The unfortunate part about it is that the factors operate insidiously. Little by little, the procedure gets a little longer. One step is added, then another, each one most thoroughly justified! Until at length we find ourselves wound up in red tape without quite knowing how it happened.

Let it be noted that procedures full of a great many steps tend to be characteristic of any big organization—government, business, industrial, or other. We cannot blindly assume that we have no such thing in *our* particular organization. The six factors operate in every organization.

Once we can honestly recognize that this sort of thing can happen here, then the problem of what to do about it is on the way to being solved. What we must do from time to time is to review critically *all* our job procedures or methods to find out whether they are indeed the best we know. We must find out whether *all* the steps are necessary, or only some; whether the steps follow one another in the right order and place; whether the procedure can be shortened, so as to make the job easier; or indeed, whether the procedure is necessary at all.

These reviews of the steps we take—the procedure we use—in getting a job done, we call work-improvement studies. In making such a study we must answer the question: Is there a simpler, easier, faster, less expensive way to do this job and still get the results we want?

This question cannot be answered by saying that the law requires it or that it is a company or agency policy. If it is clear that there is indeed a better way to do the job, were it not for laws, rules, or policy, then it is only common sense to question the validity of these impeding factors. Laws and regulations as well as policies are made by people, and they can be changed if there are sound reasons for doing so. It does not always follow that they *ought* to be changed, because there may be good reasons for them other than the way they affect job procedures. Nevertheless, *they can be changed,* and anyone making work-improvement studies must keep this in mind.

To illustrate how one might make a work-improvement study, let us consider the following simple case. If it seems somewhat ridiculous, let it be noted that red tape often looks that way to people who are not involved.

A few years ago, on a college campus, I ran across this situation. A truck had delivered a big pile of sand to the edge of a road. A worker was hauling the sand in a wheelbarrow across the lawn to a large bed of flowers and shrubs. There he spread the sand on the soil, presumably to loosen it.

The worker stopped the wheelbarrow ten feet away from the pile of sand, took the shovel, walked over to the sand pile, took a shovelful of sand, walked back to the wheelbarrow, and dumped the sand in it. He did this until the wheelbarrow was full. Then he turned the wheelbarrow around and wheeled it over to the flower bed. There he spread the sand on top of the ground.

Almost everyone is amused at such a worker. Two very obvious improvements he ought to make are:

1. Place the wheelbarrow alongside the sand, so he could shovel without walking back and forth.

2. Head it toward the flower bed before he fills it, since it is easier to turn an empty barrow than a full one.

Usually people also ask, "Why didn't the truck dump the sand at the edge of the flower bed in the first place, instead of at the edge of the road?" The answer is that the college's policy was to keep trucks off the fine lawn. Presumably, therefore, in this simple situation, about all we can do is carry out the two improvements we have already suggested, unless the college authorities agree to change their rule.

But before we give up, do any other questions occur to you? The key question here—as in all such studies—is *why?* This was the question that solved the whole problem: *Why* put sand on the flower bed? Answer: Well, it's supposed to loosen the soil. Question: Does it? Answer: No, not on this particular soil, and not as well as lime. Only a little lime would be needed, not a big pile as of the sand. As it turned out, a hundred-pound sack of lime did the job, in one trip of the wheelbarrow.

The point, of course, in this deceivingly simple situation, is that you *never take anything for granted.* Not until the necessity for the whole process was questioned did it turn out that practically all of it could be eliminated.

In making a critical and objective appraisal of any procedure, we are quite likely to encounter an apparently valid reason for what seems to be a foolish or unnecessary step. It is important that the reason be subjected to scrutiny and properly identified. If the reason is a law or policy, then consideration must be given to the advisability of changing it. If the reason is rooted in our customs or habits, we must consider how we may change these. Frequently enough, the reason for a foolish step is found to be our own misunder-standing or misinterpretation of a rule rather than the rule itself. Because this is so, we can never safely assume we know what the rule is until we carefully recheck it.

In summary, let me note that no one should undertake a work-improvement study unless he or she is prepared to take the consequences. Commonly, such studies result, or should result, in changes. If changes make you uncomfortable, do not make the study. The interesting thing about these stud-ies is that you can operate without restriction in making them. For purposes of the study you can—indeed you must—question laws, rules, policies, regulations, customs, etc. No cow is too sacred. The paramount question is to find a better way to do a job. In the end, possibly the future of the organization lies in how skillfully and systematically we make our work-improvement studies.

The People to Make the Study

By far the best way to make a work-improvement study is with the group of people who are most familiar with the procedure to be examined, that is, who regularly use the procedure. This is so for two very important reasons:

1. These people know more about the procedure than does anyone else. It is their job. Their statements are there-fore most likely to be factually correct and the least theoreti-cal.

2. These same people are the ones who will be affected if the procedure is changed. If *they* help change it, they will ac-cept the change readily enough, since it is their own doing. If someone else develops the change and tries to get them to adopt it, they are likely to find all sorts of reasons why it cannot be used. Since these people are the ones who use the procedure, they can and do nullify attempts to change it un-less there is a rigorous (and expensive) policing of the new method. With an eye to the future, therefore, enlist the ef-

forts of the people to be affected by any change. This is the easiest way to gain acceptance.

Even so, it is advisable for at least a few members of the study group to be unfamiliar with the procedure because:

a. People completely familiar with a procedure tend to accept the steps in it without question.

b. People strange to a procedure, or armed with no more than a general knowledge of it, tend to question everything about it, or to be at least more critical.

In general, the chairperson of the study group had best be someone a step removed from the users of the procedure but one who has a reasonably good knowledge of the subject. Furthermore, chairpersons must be skilled conference leaders, able to draw ideas out of the group without submerging them in their own. They must be able to stimulate objectivity and skepticism. They must be intolerant of sloppy thinking and quick to detect too ready or too tacit acceptance of invalid reasons for procedural steps. Their job is fun but it calls for quick thinking. Indeed, studies of job procedures are usually fun for everyone. After all, there are no hampering laws or policies that control the making of them.

The climate for work-improvement studies must be congenial, too. Everyone knows that tomatoes will not ripen in a dank, cold climate. They must have sun. And in making a work-improvement study, the climate must be conducive to the operation of free intelligence and good common sense. Skillful chairpersons set the stage carefully. They convince the people that they are there to try to make their job easier, that their ideas are really wanted, that they can safely question the most sacred of policies, and that mutiny, so to speak, is a good thing. The people are encouraged to ask "Why?" about every procedural detail. If at any time the chairperson's attitude seems to the participants to be censoring or condemning their ideas, the climate will become dank and cold, and new ideas are most unlikely to ripen thereafter.

The Steps in a Work-Improvement Study

A simple and practical procedure for making a work-improvement study (it, too, is a job) involves five steps, as follows:

1. Set forth clearly what the job is supposed to accomplish. This is the objective, and it acts as the standard to check against.

2. List each step in the procedure used to do the job and number it. Be sure to put in *all* the details; they have a habit of becoming important. And be sure that each step is *correctly* described.

3. Question each step in order, after they have all been listed. The whole group does this. They ask such questions as these: *Why* is it necessary? *What* purpose does it serve? Is this the best *place* to do it? The best *time?* The best *person* to do it? Isn't there a *better way* to do the step? And so on.

4. Develop a new procedure. This results rather easily from steps 2 and 3 above. All unnecessary steps are cut out, all possible details eliminated, all possible combinations of steps are made, better steps inserted, and the series is rearranged to be in the best possible order. All this is done regardless of law, policy, regulation, or what has customarily been done in the past. For future reference, we make a note of any such things that act to prevent the improvements.

5. The new procedure is either put into use as soon as practical; or if policy or regulation stand in the way, approval is sought for a change in them. If the policy or regulation can be changed by the proper authority, then the new procedure goes into effect.

An additional step ought to be put in this study procedure. This is to *evaluate* the new procedure. When steps are eliminated, it is usually possible to find out how much time is saved, how many forms are eliminated, how much filing is made unnecessary, and so on. All these things cost money. An hour a day at $2 an hour adds up to an annual cost reduction of $520. Filing space is worth several dollars per square foot. And so on. If it is necessary to get a policy or rule changed in order to install a new procedure, dollar costs provide useful arguments. Thus, between steps 4 and 5 above, we may need this evaluation step. We may also find it useful to check our estimates against actual costs *after* the new procedure is put into effect—simply to be sure that our new procedure really saves time and money.

When a Work-Improvement Study Is Needed

Many supervisors who have never undertaken such studies as these are often uncertain where and how to begin. If you feel this way, scan the following list. If any of these conditions are true in your unit, why not do a study to see if things can be made easier?

1. Too much paperwork.
2. Too much red tape.
3. Too many copies required of this or that form or report, or too many forms or reports.
4. Too many mistakes being made.
5. Procedures too cumbersome.
6. Operations that seem to take more time than they should.
7. Costs too high.
8. Too much waste.
9. A bottleneck slowing things down.

It is seldom that a supervisor can say none of these things are true of a unit. If you feel this way, you had better ask your people. They may have a different idea.

Experience in many organizations shows clearly that no matter how efficient a procedure may seem, you had better restudy it after no more than three years. Procedures tend to get more complex. Furthermore, times change and so do people. Enough change takes place in three years to warrant review of any procedure. If your procedures have not been studied for five years, chances are they can be much improved.

Experienced supervisors have found that devoting a few hours of their entire group's time to such studies regularly, once a month, can pay dividends. If, say, on the first Monday (or any other day that suits), everyone stops regular work and goes at a work-improvement study, there is hope for greater efficiency. This also enables all the people to participate—and as we have already seen, this pays.

15

Solving Problem Cases

If all supervisors started their unit from the beginning, and did a topnotch job of supervision thereafter, presumably they would never have a serious personnel problem. At least, many supervisors seem to believe this. They will tell you that they have inherited the people in their unit, along with various problems, and they imply that this is scarcely their fault. Sometimes supervisors are inclined to shrug their shoulders over these inherited problems. "Let personnel take care of it," they say. "This is none of my doing."

Of course, nearly all supervisors do inherit their people, just as the people of a unit often inherit their supervisor. Indifference to the human problems that come along with the people denotes a supervisor unwilling to face realities or unable to solve problems any supervisor must expect to have to deal with sooner or later. Nor is starting with a clean slate a guarantee that problems will not arise. Personnel problems can sprout and grow anywhere, any time. They are usually much harder to solve if they are permitted to go on for a long time. It is far better if they can be nipped in the bud in their early stages.

The curious thing is that the beginnings of a problem case can easily go unrecognized, often for quite a while. Such cases seem characteristically to assume unexpected size before some supervisors recognize them for what they are. The sooner these developing cases can be distinguished, the simpler their solution may turn out to be. Experienced (and capable) supervisors learn to spot symptoms that may be indicative of a developing problem. They can often "sense" such a development because of their thorough knowledge of their people, the work they do, and the general principles of supervision they use in their work.

A suggestion to new supervisors: The symptoms usually consist of some kind of *change* in the attitude, work habits, or behavior of an individual. For example, a person begins to come late for work, not just once but often. Two people in the unit stop speaking to each other. A person develops a habit of staring out the window. A worker, formerly doing good work, begins turning out sloppy work. These symptoms and many others like them are small matters, but they may indicate something is wrong.

There are two courses of action good supervisors should not take when confronted with a problem case. They should not try to solve it by transferring the case out of their unit. Transfer of a problem child, except as a bona fide move toward better placement, is the mark of inexperience or ineptitude. Unfortunately, there are plenty of supervisors who try this first, without ever seeking to solve the problem where it has arisen. This practice should be condemned wherever it occurs. It denotes a shirking of a primary responsibility that is inherent in the job of every supervisor.

The second course supervisors should not take is to dump the case in the lap of personnel staff people the moment they recognize the problem. It is a familiar and plaintive cry of the inept supervisor that personnel or civil service ought to *do* something. The staff people of a personnel office cannot be responsible for all the problem cases that arise. They are there to provide expert advice and counsel to supervisors, but the responsibility for dealing with the problem is first of all with the supervisor.

Some Suggested Approaches

Certain general rules must be kept in mind when we approach a problem case, big or little. These rules, or ideas, can help a supervisor to avoid many mistakes, although they cannot be used as a guarantee of success. Some of these ideas have already been noted in Chapter 2, but here we will expand and illustrate their use.

1. Possibly the first question to be answered is whether the supervision itself has been adequate. Conscientious supervisors owe it to themselves and their people to ask themselves just such a question when a problem arises that may cast doubt on the quality of the supervisory job they have done so far. A useful checklist to consider would include the seven principles of supervision discussed in Chapter 2, like this:

a. Do the workers really understand clearly what is expected of them? *How do we know this?*

b. Have they really been given appropriate guidance in doing their work? *Sure about this?*

c. Has their good work been recognized? *All of it? When?*

d. Have they been given constructive help in improving their poor work? *When? What happened?*

e. Have they ever been given a real opportunity to show that they can do more responsible work than their position calls for? *How did they do?*

f. In what specific way have they been encouraged to improve themselves? *What did they do?*

g. Are their working conditions really satisfactory? *Which ones are? Which ones are not?*

If a supervisor cannot give positive answers to these questions, after careful and thoughtful consideration, then it is possible that the correction of any omissions may help solve the case. First of all, that is, the use of supervisory principles must be correct and complete. Incidentally, supervisors may find it useful to review this question with their own supervisors, as impartially as they are able. Sometimes they may learn that they do not see the application of supervisory methods in the same way that their supervisor does. They should make no attempt here to alibi their work but rather to enlist help in evaluating their efforts up to date.

2. A second question of great importance is whether the problem case, that is, the human being concerned, is well and fully known. Specifically, a supervisor must review such questions as these:

a. What about the employee's past history with the organization? What are the facts about employment, transfers, promotions, performance, and qualifications for the present job?

b. Are there any pertinent facts about the person's home life? Is there any trouble financially? With his family? From the standpoint of health? In any other way? How do we know this?

c. What facts do we have about the worker's interest in the work, attitudes, and ambitions?

Our point here is to be sure that an employee's background and experience are generally pretty well known. Recognizing that we cannot possibly know everything about it, we should still be clear about the salient facts. Unless this is so, trying to solve a problem involving the individual may be more difficult or impossible.

3. Next we come to the question that is frequently the most important one of all, namely, "Why?" Why has the person done or failed to do the things in question? Why does the person have a negative attitude? Why does the worker seem to lack ambition? Why is the work poor? Why has the person failed?

Over and over again, an answer to the question "Why?" may give a clue to successful action. If we are not sure of the reasons underlying employee behavior, our efforts to improve it are not likely to be particularly successful. Unless we undertake to find out why employees have done what they have done, or failed to do what we wanted them to, we may find ourselves condemning them unjustly. We may, in fact, start to take action that has little to do with the real problem. In 1949 Bruce Stewart, writing in *Science*,[1] pointed out:

> We have not yet realized the full significance of the elementary principle that there are causes for social phenomena. If we applied that principle, we would renounce such attitudes as blame or condemnation of sin. These attitudes lead us away from an attack on causes, and therefore away from cure and prevention of human ills. No physicist would kick his apparatus because it didn't work right.

4. As a sort of corollary, it is of great importance that the supervisor *talk* with problem children. Many cases can be resolved if supervisors can only encourage such individuals to talk. This means, as we have noted in Chapter 11, that the supervisor must be skilled in the art of listening.

Frequently the only source of the answer to our "Why?" question are the problem cases, that is, the human beings. They may not always know why they are acting as they do, but sometimes they know very well. Being human, they may offer many reasons tending to vindicate their attitude or excuse their failure, but if they can be led to talk it out, in the end both they and the supervisor may come to understand the reasons underlying the undesired behavior.

Too many supervisors seem fearful of talking freely with their problem children. They seem to consider it an uncomfortable or distasteful thing to do. But it is not. Not, that is, if the supervisor is seeking to understand. Then it becomes a very interesting and worthwhile thing to do.

We can summarize a number of these points in simple chart form, setting forth useful do's and don'ts. These are based on the experience of a great many successful supervisors.

1. *Science*, vol. 110, p. 82, 1949.

Do:	Don't:
1. Check your own supervision	1. Ignore small problems
2. Check your knowledge of the person	2. Try to dump the case in the lap of personnel
3. Ask *why*	3. Try to transfer the case just to get rid of it
4. Talk with the person about the problem	4. Treat symptoms; rather, search for the cause

Before we look at a few interesting cases, let us note that our discussion so far has placed a great deal of responsibility on the supervisor. We suggest that people who hope to become proficient in supervision may welcome this responsibility. We suggest also that those who seek to avoid it are well advised to go into some other kind of work.

The cases we discuss below are all described from real life. We have selected them as illustrative of a few of the more common problems, problems that are most likely to confront supervisors. However, no case you may have will prove to be exactly like these, and chances are good that you may have a case quite unlike any of them. Furthermore, for reasons of space and to bring out points as sharply as possible, all the full surrounding factors in each case have generally been omitted. We concentrate primarily on facts and factors that had most to do with the problem and its solution.

The Case of the Tardy File Clerk

This problem began in a very simple way, as such cases often do. The vivacious, attractive woman of twenty-five, who worked as a clerk in the filing section of a huge government office, began coming late to work. This was somewhat distressing to all concerned, because the woman was so well liked. Eventually the supervisor called her in, told her this sort of thing could not be tolerated, and warned her to be on time thereafter. For a few days, the file clerk got to work on time. Then she began coming late again.

Over a period of time, despite repeated warnings, she was late to work, and in addition she took too much time for coffee breaks and lunch. The supervisor began to charge her with leave for these periods and spoke to her very strongly about the matter many times. The supervisor even went over bus schedules with the woman to show her how to get to work at starting time. None of this helped. Finally, the supervisor began to think of discharging her, since her actions were having a decidedly adverse effect on the rest of the people in the unit.

At this point the supervisor sought advice. What should be done? "Everything" had been tried; nothing had worked. Was it not obvious that the woman would have to be discharged? Open-and-shut case, it looked like. But was it?

Careful review and checking on the facts revealed the following points:

1. Our personable file clerk had a college degree in languages. The supervisor did not know this; the personnel file had not been checked.

2. She was fully adept in the use of several foreign languages. This was in the file, too, but the supervisor did not know it. She could have found out by reference to the file or by talking to the woman, or both.

3. The woman took the clerical job because she could not find anything else. She became bored with it and demonstrated as clearly as possible that she really was not interested in the work she was doing. This, too, the supervisor did not know or realize.

4. All this came to light when the supervisor, *for the first time*, actually sat down and *listened* to what the woman had to say. Before this the supervisor had done all the talking— aimed at getting her to work on time, nothing else.

The upshot of the case was that the supervisor sought the

help of staff personnel people. They arranged the woman's transfer to a department where foreign language facility was in demand. Placed in work she enjoyed and was trained for, the "file clerk" did a good job.

In this case the supervisor was unable to solve the case primarily because she made no effort to do anything other than to cure the symptom, lateness to work. She neglected to learn all she could about this particular one of her people. She assumed too much without checking even those facts readily available. And possibly worst of all, she never had a full discussion with her file clerk about her work, her background, her ambitions, her lack of interest in filing—that is, she forgot to ask, "Why?"

You may consider this an unusual case, with a too-dramatic ending. And perhaps it is. But let us hasten to note that every case is unusual, even if the solution may not prove as dramatic as in this one. You may consider, too, that the supervisor in this case must have been quite inexperienced, and this is correct. The supervisor had had only a couple of years' experience and no training whatever for the job she was doing. With due regard for these facts, however, let us note that observed defects in a person's work are symptoms; that we must seek to find the underlying reasons for undesirable behavior; and that every case has depth to it, often extending far below the observed symptoms.

In this case we see also that a good job of placement may be of great help. Note, however, that placement was not used to get rid of a tardy file clerk, but to get a qualified language specialist into a suitable position. Actually the problem was well on the way to solution before placement was considered.

The Case of the Distracted Field Man

This problem has to do with a young man of thirty-eight who worked in an office in a small town and who had been working for the same organization for fifteen years. He had a wife and several children, an excellent record in his work, and was well liked by his associates. Then, without apparent reason, his work began to deteriorate. He forgot things he should have remembered to do, failed to meet his goals, generally went downhill. His supervisor noted this early in the game and made every attempt he could think of to find out why. His record—carefully reviewed—was impeccable. In the meantime, the man became irritable and difficult to talk to. He became curt and abrupt with the public with whom he had to deal every day. After a number of progressively worse months, the supervisor decided in some desperation to recommend his discharge. The record was clear; the man was simply not performing up to reasonable standards, despite his previous fine work; he showed no improvement after repeated attempts to talk with him and help him. The supervisor felt he could not put up with the situation any longer since, after all, there was a job to be done. So the supervisor took the whole story to his boss and they talked it all over.

The two supervisors found, after careful and lengthy review, that there was simply nothing that could account for the failure of the man. And undoubtedly this was their most significant finding. People do not do things for no reason at all; behind every facet of a human being's behavior there is a cause, if it can only be found. This was the way the two supervisors reasoned. Then they took action—not to discharge the man or penalize him but to get at the reason behind the failure. The man himself, as a source of information, was by this time unsatisfactory. He had become somewhat sullen and definitely uncommunicative. So the supervisors quietly went to other sources—to the man's associates, to his friends, and finally to his wife. They explained their sincere desire to help the man, that they were trying to discover how they might help him, that they were sure he needed help, but that they were baffled by his unwillingness to cooperate with them. They knew this was uncertain ground; the news was almost sure to get back to the man that they were "checking on him." But they felt their man's record was far too good to be thrown away as wasted.

To make a long story short, they uncovered the fact that the man had made a bad investment financially and was too proud to admit it. His purchase had been unwise; his family security was jeopardized; his preoccupation with the problem had distracted the attention he had formerly given to his job. The effect on the man has already been described. Armed with this information, the two supervisors met with the man and explained sympathetically that they knew about his trouble and wanted to help. The man blustered, denied it, then threw up his hands and admitted the whole thing with considerable emotion. In later consultation the banker holding a mortgage on the property proved willing to cooperate. The property was finally disposed of with very little loss to our distracted employee, and his work righted itself in due course.

In this case we note the need for persistence in getting an answer to "Why?" that makes sense. We also note that supervisors may, on occasion, have to go to considerable lengths to be sure of their facts. How far to go, of course, depends on the situation. Here, an excellent fifteen-year record obviously justified more than ordinary supervisor effort.

The Case of the New Concept

Our next case can best be told in three brief episodes that took place over a period of half-a-dozen months. The story unfolded in a supervisory training course in which a group of supervisors were studying and discussing much of the material in this book. Early in the course the men were reviewing the various factors important in creating job satisfaction or dissatisfaction. The discussion stemmed from the results of the Pittsburgh study described in Chapter 7. One of the supervisors was a newly appointed foreman of a large group of men in an electric products manufacturing plant. He was voicing his opinion:

"All this stuff may be okay, but I still say it's money that means the most to people. What can you do without money? That's what pays the bills. That's what people go to work for in the first place." He extended his hand and rubbed forefinger against thumb in the ancient gesture. "I say it's cash makes the world go round, and that first and foremost it's pay that motivates people to work."

The second incident developed two months later. In the meantime, each supervisor had been asked to bring in a problem for discussion. This time it was the turn of our electric products foreman. His problem had to do with getting production in his unit.

"I'm fairly new on my job," he was saying, "but I'm expected to show results. And so far, I'm just not getting them. My men don't seem to be interested in trying to turn out more work, and they couldn't care less whether we're doing better or worse this month than we did last month." What could he do to get his men to work with him?

The other supervisors in the group started probing. Had he put the production problem up to the men? Had he tried to get their participation in solving it? What had he done to gain his men's confidence? Had he shown them in any way that he had confidence in *them?*

No, it turned out, he had done none of these things. His idea was still clear, that well-paid people could be expected to be high-producing—as a matter of course. "And don't think my men aren't paid well," he went on. "They get as high pay as you can get in the business, and there's plenty of bonuses and fringe benefits besides. It just doesn't make sense the way they're not trying."

The discussion went on. How was the quality of the work? If the quantity was low, was the quality, too? On this point, the young foreman was emphatic that at least some of the work being done was first class. He described an exceptionally good design that one of his men had produced only recently.

One of the supervisors in the group asked if the fine job had been recognized in any way. "Well," the foreman said, "I told him he was putting out the kind of work we expected around here." But was the job good enough to write to him about it? Why not put it in writing and get it in the man's record?

Two months later, in the ending sessions of the course, the third part of the story unfolded. When our foreman asked permission to "say a few words," he had difficulty getting started, but he developed enthusiasm as he went along.

"Look," he started, "you guys were telling me a while back about writing letters to men in my outfit who did a good job. I didn't think the idea was very good, but I finally figured what could I lose, so I wrote a couple. I sent one to the fellow I was telling you about—the one who turned out a design that was probably one of the best my outfit ever came up with. And I wrote another one to an old-timer we had, telling him I appreciated his advice about a tough circuit problem we had, and that when we took his advice, things worked out pretty good. Like you guys suggested, I sent a copy of both letters to my boss, who's in charge of our division, and to the personnel office.

"And you know what?" the young foreman exclaimed. "It worked! My boss called me in later on and told me I was doing all right. But the best thing is that my men are working better. It isn't just the production sheets we get either; you can feel it around the office. And besides this," he went on, "I've got the old-timer on my side now, and we're working on the idea of having the men meet once a month to go over how we're doing and how we can do better."

There was more. But there are several points to note. One is that the company itself obviously was encouraging enlightened supervision—both because the foreman was being sent to the supervisory course, and because the foreman's boss commended his action. Another is that when the old concepts—such as "money makes the world go round"—do not work, what, indeed, is there to lose by trying newer concepts based on scientific study? Actually the foreman took a step in the new direction that is probably easier to take than almost any other—he began by expressing his appreciation of good work by according recognition where it was deserved. We do not know about the many factors operating in the foreman's group of people, of course, but we may note that sincere praise is something that can break down many barriers.

Illustrated here is the simple fact, long known from many studies, that a supervisor operating on the basis of unfounded opinion about what people want from their jobs is likely to experience trouble. Once he proceeds on a corrected basis, and does so sincerely, he is likely to begin experiencing a new and different kind of response from his people.

The Case of the Young Man in Trouble

Here we have a young man of twenty-seven who has a wife and a little boy. He had been five years with a government agency and had a satisfactory record and was doing good work. Then one day, his supervisor got a phone call from a local department store. The young man owed quite a bill, and had not paid anything on it despite repeated letters. Could the supervisor do anything about this?

The supervisor agreed to talk to the man and see if she could get things straightened out. This she did. Our young man was embarrassed. He explained that he had bought a new house recently and was a little hard put financially to take care of everything when it was due, but that he would try to take care of the bill at once.

A few weeks later another creditor called. Payments were

overdue. Could the government do anything? More discussion with the young man brought on more embarrassment and another promise to take care of the payments.

Over a period of several months, a number of calls came in, all from creditors, asking that the man pay his long-overdue bills. The latest discussion between the supervisor and the young man brought out that (1) he had contracted to pay more for his house than he could really afford, (2) he and his wife together owed local merchants much more than they could pay, and (3) he and his wife had separated in the meantime. All told, our young man was in considerable difficulty.

Government supervisors with a case like this on their hands face a perplexing dilemma. The man frequently has a good record, does good work, and is officially a desirable man to keep. However, his personal affairs are obviously not well handled, and worse, they become embarrassing to the agency. How should the supervisor proceed?

This question cannot be answered quickly and easily for several reasons. First, the government will not garnishee wages or salaries in order to pay creditors. Second, the "official" government policy with respect to employees in financial difficulties varies with the agency. In agencies where security is of great importance, nonpayment of legitimate debts may be cause for instant dismissal—a bad security risk. In other agencies, a more lenient attitude is taken; employees are given every reasonable opportunity to get their financial affairs arranged, so that they do not interfere with official business. If this cannot be done, the employee is ultimately asked to resign. Failing this, the employee is discharged.

In this specific case, the young man's supervisor was able to talk over the entire problem with him. It turned out that the total amount of money owed was a large sum, more than the young man could borrow. It also came out that the separation of the employee and his wife was in the hands of lawyers, and that disposing of the home was out of the question until settlement could be effected. It became clear ultimately that the young man's judgment had not been good and that he had placed himself in jeopardy through a series of quite unwise and even irresponsible decisions. In the end, he was asked to resign and did so rather than have his record show dismissal.

Let us note that this action was taken by the supervisor with great reluctance. The supervisor was aware that the young man needed help—even as he was being asked to resign. The loss of his job put the young man in even worse trouble. This was a hard decision for the supervisor to make and for the personnel staff people who were called in to give expert advice. The government, however, cannot tolerate actions by its employees that tend to discredit or embarrass the agency. The young man really had no one to blame but himself. He had an indulgent supervisor who tried personally to assist him in every possible way open to him. He chose personally to pursue a course that led eventually to his own disaster.

The Case of the Religious Candidate

Here we have a government office that was required by the nature of its work to operate every Saturday in addition to the regular five days during the week. Each weekend, in rotation, one of the three supervisors of the unit was expected to be on duty. At the time of this particular case, one of the supervisory jobs was vacant, and there were two candidates for the job.

The first candidate on the promotion list was somewhat better qualified than the second, although both were very good men. The job was accordingly offered to the first candidate, who was quite willing to take it. He stipulated, however, that he would not work on Saturday because his religion prevented him from doing so. After full discussion of the situation with him, it became clear that (1) there was no other way the work could be arranged except to perform part of it on Saturday, and (2) because of this, the first candidate could not undertake the job. The job was therefore offered to the second candidate, who accepted it and was entirely willing to undertake the necessary Saturday work.

Our first candidate thereupon claimed unfair treatment on the grounds that (1) he was the best-qualified man on the promotion list and (2) he was being discriminated against because of his religion. He threatened to appeal the case to the Office of Personnel Management, and because of the religious factor, the supervisor of the unit became fearful of possible consequences.

Now it is true that religious discrimination may not be tolerated in the government service. In this case, however, there was clearly no such discrimination, since the protesting candidate had been offered the position ahead of his nearest competitor and had, indeed, been urged to take it. The candidate had refused the job because his religion did not permit him to work on Saturday. Clearly, it was the candidate who had disqualified himself. There was no discrimination on the part of his agency.

The Case of the Supervisor Who Got What She Deserved

A group of twelve people who were stationed in a small city were working on an activity that required at least two employees to be on duty all the time. They had a schedule that provided for a rotation of employees among day, evening, and night shifts. The supervisor had arranged this schedule so that she worked only during the daytime and only Monday through Friday. Her people did the rotating.

Official policy of the agency required all employees to meet certain academic requirements in order to advance above a certain level. Furthermore, the agency encouraged its employees to take college courses that would help qualify them for a promotion. Fortunately, in the city where our unit was, a college offered day and evening classes in exactly the right subjects.

Our problem case developed when two of the employees asked for permission to take one of the college courses. It seemed that the college required regular attendance in the classes. Because of the schedule of rotation among shifts, they could not meet attendance requirements. They were quite willing to be assigned either to day, evening, or night shifts during the school year if they did not have to rotate from one shift to another. Could this be arranged?

Our unit supervisor commended the employees on their ambition but was dubious about the effect of assigning them to regular shifts. She must be fair to all her employees, she said, and to be sure everyone was satisfied, she would put the matter to a vote. This she did.

The vote count showed five employees in favor of the idea and six against it. Hence the two employees had to keep on rotating among shifts and, of course, were unable to go to school. The majority, it seemed, was opposed to any further education.

The two employees promptly requested transfers elsewhere and shortly thereafter got them. People to replace them were hard to find, and several months passed before they were finally recruited and their training begun. In the meantime, the entire staff had to carry additional work, take the more difficult shifts until the new men were trained, and work various unscheduled shifts. Things even got so bad that the supervisor herself had to work many nights and on some of the weekends!

We may consider that what happened to the supervisor and her "majority" served them right. But of course, the minority had to do extra work also, and the effect in total on the people of the unit and on the work itself was bad. Here we have a supervisor who failed to exert leadership. What she should have done was ask her people, "How can we arrange this?" The agency policy was already clear: employees were to be encouraged to take college courses. The schedule could have been rearranged to permit the two men to attend college; and the rearrangement would in itself have been evidence to the rest of the employees that they, too, could go to school if they wanted to go badly enough.

The Case of the End Run

The head of a section with a dozen people in it was promoted to the position of director of the division. Everyone in his old unit liked him and had confidence in him. They hated to see him go, but they were all pleased at his advancement. They got a new supervisor, one of themselves.

The division director was now supervising half-a-dozen section heads, including the new supervisor of his old unit. He was a very busy man, but never too busy to forget his "old bunch." From time to time, one of them dropped in, to his delight, talked over how things were going, brought up a problem or two, chatted awhile.

In the meantime, the new section head of the director's old unit was working at keeping things rolling as well as his former boss did. He was new, and he lacked experience, but he tried hard to gain the confidence of his people. After a time, he noticed that some of his men seemed to know more than he did about what was going on. They were often ready with answers about what to do—they got them from the old boss, now division director. Gradually, our new section head realized that the division director really had not quite given up supervising his old unit. Men in the section were making end runs directly to the old boss and he was going along with this kind of operation. Knowing that some of his men were very good friends with the old boss, the new section head felt frustrated about what to do. If he tried to stop them, they would go to the old boss who was now his supervisor. If he let them go on short-cutting him, he would never gain control of his unit.

In the real-life case, the new section head put up with the end runs, hoping that eventually they would end. But they did not, and our section head became more frustrated than ever, then bitter. After a good many months, he was sullen and suspicious of his men and of his supervisor, the old boss; he was ready to quit.

What the new section head should have done was to lay the whole matter before his supervisor just as soon as he realized what was going on. He should have explained why the end runs were defeating him and how this would, in the end, cause difficulty in the whole division. As it happened, the division director would have been glad to cooperate, if he had only realized. By and large, most supervisors of any experience would. The solution to the problem required that cooperation.

If there is any moral here, it is that the longer a problem is let go, the worse it may get. All supervisors, new or experienced, must face up to their problems just as soon as they are sure of their ground. Then they must take the best action they can. If the action calls for considerable diplomacy, as this one seemed to, then they should take that kind of action. But whatever they do, they should never let the problem fester and get worse.

The Case of the Up-and-Down Windows

Simple as this case may be, it happens over and over again in countless offices. The usual situation is that there are six to twelve people in a room. Of these, one or two are very sensitive to drafts and want the office warm; one or two others like it cool and prefer plenty of fresh air. The rest of the people usually do not care one way or another. When this situation includes both men and women of various ages and habits, trouble often starts.

One of the men, for instance, begins by opening a window. In a few minutes one of the women marches over and shuts it. Later the man opens it again. And again the woman shuts it. This process seems only amusing at first. Later it gets to be a nuisance. As time goes on, the people may form themselves into two groups—the ups and the downs. In certain long-continued situations, the work is seriously interrupted and the people get angry with each other.

Supervisors must see that these silly-simple cases do not develop, or if they have already developed and are running out of control, that they are stopped. There are various ways to do this, depending on the people, but possibly the best way is to get the whole group together and put the problem up to them. Try for agreement, but get compromises if agreement is not forthcoming. Then try what the whole groups suggests. Frequently this works, but if it does not, then here is one way that usually does:

1. Put the people who dislike the open windows as far away from the windows as possible.

2. Put the open-air people right next to the windows.

3. Get a thermometer and place it in the center of the room. Get an agreement (or a compromise) on the best temperature—say 70°F.

4. Anyone can look at the thermometer, but only the supervisor takes action to open or close the windows.

The Case of the Passed-Over Candidate

This is the familiar situation in which one person out of three is promoted, and the two unsuccessful candidates complain of unfair treatment, prejudice, office politics, or other skulduggery. Depending on circumstances, there are many ways to deal with this situation, but one thing is very clear: *the supervisor must deal with it.*

The unsuccessful candidates are now unhappy about their jobs because of what they consider unsatisfactory personnel policy. This is a dissatisfier factor, as noted in Chapter 7. You may not think their attitude is justified, but this is beside the point: they are dissatisfied.

Now there must have been a reason or reasons why you chose one person ahead of the other two. This could have been because of differences in ability or personality, or because of judgment about the others' potentiality for development in the new job. The problem is to convince the unsuccessful employees on about five points:

1. That you believe all three are good workers.

2. That the job called for certain specific qualifications, as well as a certain personality and potential.

3. That the person you chose came closest to these needs.

4. That for each of the trailing candidates you have in mind (or better, on paper) some additional training and development that will help prepare them for the next opportunity.

5. That you need them, and that you need their support for the person promoted, if this is required.

The Case of the Two Poor Supervisors

Joe, one of a number of engineers in an office, comes in one morning to urge his supervisor to consider a change in construction of a satellite part. He suggests using a single copper wire coated with silver instead of a twelve-strand copper wire, to be conducted in a single insulated tube instead of two tubes, as used heretofore. (The suggestion is technically sound.)

He points out that this change will save weight, space, money, and materials. His supervisor is dubious. "We've always done it with two tubes and copper wire," he says, "and we're getting along fine."

At this point the supervisor's boss comes in, overhears part of the discussion, jumps to the conclusion that Joe is resisting a change being recommended by his supervisor. He speaks strongly to Joe, advising him that his attitude is not good, that useful changes *are* desirable, and that Joe must accept new ideas gracefully. Joe's supervisor says nothing; in fact, he seldom supports his people. The supervisor's boss then leaves. Whereupon Joe turns on his supervisor and tells him what he thinks of his failure to explain what really was happening and leaves in a huff.

This case is well-packed with errors. Joe himself made a mistake when he turned on his supervisor, even though he had good reason. Joe's supervisor failed to clarify the situation when *his* boss was speaking strongly to the wrong man. The supervisor's boss was also in error when he undertook to correct Joe; this, if necessary, was up to Joe's supervisor. Besides this, the supervisor's boss apparently jumps to conclusions pretty quickly.

In the meantime, after Joe had a chance to cool off, he realized he was in a bad spot. No more promotions for him, since the two supervisors controlled these. If he quit and tried to get another job, wherever he applied, inquiries would be made of his last company. He would not get a good reference, obviously. If he tried to see his supervisor's boss and straighten out the situation, he'd get his supervisor in trouble, and this wouldn't help. Probably he made a mistake in not speaking up when his supervisor failed to do so. But the events took place quickly, and Joe kept thinking surely his supervisor would say something. The company is a relatively new one. It has no suggestion system yet. And there is no union. As Joe thought it over, it became clear that he couldn't simply do nothing.

What actually happened was that Joe and his fellow engineers decided they had enough of a supervisor who never supported his people. So in a body, they went directly to the supervisor's boss and demanded the removal of the supervisor. They would *all* quit unless this change were made. Since engineers were rather hard to get at the time, the supervisor's boss agreed to do as they demanded. And in a short time, he got the supervisor out. Interestingly enough, he did the job awkwardly, and such a rumpus was raised, that the company replaced *him* also!

You may or may not agree with this solution. It is worthwhile, though, to study the mistakes. It is unnecessary for a situation like this one to develop—providing a supervisor is performing as a good supervisor should.

16

Books and Journals

As we noted in the first chapter of this book, supervisors who hope to do a professional job of supervision must do a certain amount of reading. They must know the best books in the field and must be able to evaluate them. Furthermore, they should see the more important professional magazines or journals, both to learn of new ideas and to pick up information about new books recently published.

We start first with some of the books. They are listed in alphabetical order by the author's or editor's name. This list is a starter set of books that most supervisors will find of value. Many of them have been referred to elsewhere in this book.

Useful Books for Supervisors

"Japanese Technology Today" by James C. Abbeglen and Akio Etori. *Scientific American,* October 1982. It is labeled as an advertisement and consists of 31 pages, beginning with its own cover in color. It follows page 84 of the October *Scientific American,* and contains a few advertisements of its own.

The article is of considerable importance to American managers and supervisors. It deals with robots, microelectronics, unions, older workers, automation, word processing, and other subjects, all in pungent, simple language. Explanations are given for Japanese successes in these areas. Interviews are included with twenty-two managers of important Japanese organizations, such as Sony, Toyota, Honda, Sanyo, Matsushita, Mitsubishi, and numerous others, including fifteen additional companies in America and England.

Management and the Worker, The Japanese Solutions, by James C. Abbeglen. New York: Harper & Row, 1973.

The author made a comprehensive report on management in Japan that is good reading along with Vogel's book. The author is vice-president and director of the Boston Consulting Group, and concurrently is professor of international management at Sophia University in Tokyo. His many books on Japan are authoritative.

Roads to Agreement, by Stuart Chase, with Marian Tyler Chase. New York: Harper & Row, 1951, 250 pages.

In this book Chase has put together all the techniques he could find that might help people to reach agreement. He draws from many scientific fields as well as experience. He borrows from conciliations of labor disputes, unanimous jury agreements, and Quaker meetings. How can we work together? How can we improve our relations with each other? He tries to answer questions such as these by describing how such things have been done, here and there, by all sorts of people and groups.

If you are not familiar with the clear writing and easy style of this author, you should be. (See especially his *Men at Work* and *The Proper Study of Mankind.*)

The Practice of Management, by Peter F. Drucker. New York: Harper & Row, 1954. 404 pages.

Most of the articles or books written by Peter Drucker, of New York University, are highly stimulating. This book is one of his best. You may not always agree with what he says, but he will make you think. He takes delight in reducing to a shambles some of the comfortable ideas one gets from textbooks, as well as our unsupported assumptions and beliefs.

Emphasis and examples here are from business and industrial organizations. Worth reading a number of times. Readers should be warned that Drucker's writing is brilliant, but that no one should be misled by Drucker's emphatic statements into believing that everything he says is gospel.

Motivation Through the Work Itself, by Robert N. Ford. New York: American Management Association, 1969.

A full report of the installation and use of Herzberg's motivational concepts at Bell Telephone. The study deals with the use of the satisfier factors, and the work was performed in a scientific way. The results included increased productivity, reduced turnover, fewer absences from work, fewer employee grievances, and the like. A very important piece of work, and one that merits close study by supervisors.

Motivation and Productivity, by Saul Gellerman. New York: American Management Association, 1963. 304 pages.

A well-written summary (up to 1963) of the contributions of psychology and sociology to management.

The Motivation to Work, by Frederick Herzberg, Bernard Mausner, and Barbara Bloch Snyderman. New York: Wiley, 1959. 157 pages.

Possibly one of the most important studies in the field of supervision in recent years. A full discussion of this study is found in Chapter 7.

Work and the Nature of Man, by Frederick Herzberg. New York: World, 1966. 203 pages.

Summarizes the foregoing book and relates the later findings concerning the Motivator-Hygiene theory of motivation. Treated in Chapter 7 of this book.

Bureaucracy, by J. M. Juran. New York: Harper & Row, 1944. 138 pages.

This little book has been out of print for a while, but it will probably not be out of date for many years to come. In it an industrial engineer considers how the government could be improved through the application of known management techniques. He suggests that half as many people as were employed when he wrote the book could do the needed work, but that to achieve this would take years. He proposes five basic ideas that might help to bring this about, and some of these are, indeed, gradually permeating the federal government.

Juran understands, as many industrial engineers do not, the reasons underlying government operation. Furthermore, he sees the parallels in industry. He pokes fun at both government and industry, but gently, and will full sympathy for the underlying causes. This book is a delight to read. It leaves its readers at once amused and thoughtful. Get it from your library.

How to Talk with People, by Irving J. Lee. New York: Harper & Row, 1952. 176 pages.

A book of great value for its treatment of the talking-listening process. Some of the ideas in this book can be found in Chapter 11. Contains an excellent discussion of people's behavior in conferences and of ways for people to reach agreement. The first chapter is a ten-page summary of what is in the book, but do not stop with this. Ideas spill out of every page in the book. Note especially the little gem labeled Chapter IX, which deals with the soft approach to an argument. Easy reading, but requires close attention and careful study to be sure you have wrung the last drop out of the material. Some statements are so simply put that you can easily miss the brilliant core of truth in them.

It is worth noting that Lee made six half-hour motion pictures before his death in 1955. In these he discusses simply but brilliantly the factors that lead to misunderstanding when people talk together. The title of one of the pictures is

Why Do People Misunderstand Each Other?, and it is a good one to start with. The films are distributed by the Net Film Service, Indiana University, Bloomington, Indiana. A note to them will bring a folder describing the six films, and telling where you can rent or buy them.

The Human Organization: Its Management and Value, by Rensis Likert. New York: McGraw-Hill, 1967. 258 pages.

Contains the results of research in many companies and organizations over a period of more than twenty years. Treated briefly on pp. 108–110. A most important set of ideas about participation as well as organization.

New Ways of Managing Conflict, by Rensis Likert and Jane Gibson Likert. New York: McGraw-Hill, 1976. 375 pages.

An up-to-date treatment of the participative system and its use in resolving conflict.

A New Approach to Industrial Economics, by James F. Lincoln. New York: Devin-Adair, 1961. 166 pages.

A remarkable book about the Lincoln Electric Company of Cleveland. Discussed in Chapter 6.

The Failure of Success, by Alfred T. Marrow. New York: American Management Association, 1972. 339 pages.

Of special value in its description of participation and its relation to organization operation and changes.

Making Management Human, by Alfred J. Marrow. New York: McGraw-Hill, 1957. 241 pages.

An exceptionally well-written and interesting book, full of useful and practical ideas for supervisors. Emphasis, as noted in the title, is on the human aspects of management. Has a good bit on participation, and treats the subject in a most illuminating way. Also contains good discussions on why people work; incentives; and communications. Illustrated and enlivened by a series of amusing cartoons taken from many sources and poking a little fun at various aspects of management.

The Human Side of Enterprise, by Douglas McGregor. New York: McGraw-Hill, 1960. 246 pages.

This is a book that is worth a great deal of thoughtful study. The ideas in it are important. They have had a major effect on the field of management. A brief résumé of McGregor's theory X and theory Y and their application to management is given in Chapter 9, beginning on page 105.

Japanese Society, by Chie Nakane. Berkeley: University of California Press, 1972.

An in-depth treatment of groups in Japan. See especially pages 19 and 86.

Theory Z., How American Business Can Meet the Japanese Challenge, by William Ouchi. Reading, Mass.: Addison-Wesley, 1981. 283 pages.

Theory Z., as Ouchi points out, suggests that involved workers are the key to increased productivity. We need "to manage people in such a way that they can work together more effectively. Theory Z offers several such ways." The first five chapters and the conclusion are particularly useful.

The Art of Japanese Management, Applications for American Executives, by Richard Tanner Pascale and Anthony G. Athos. New York: Warner, 1981.

Pascale of Stanford and Athos of Harvard present a comparison of Japanese management and that of the United States. "Without a doubt," they write, "the most significant outcome of the way Japanese organizations manage themselves is that to a far greater extent than in the United States they get everyone in the organization to be alert, to look for opportunities to do things better, and to strive by virtue of each small contribution to make the company succeed" (p. 305).

For Harmony and Strength, by Thomas P. Rohlen. Berkeley: University of California Press, 1979. 285 pages. (Published under the auspices of the Center for Japanese and Korean Studies.)

Essential for a full understanding of Japanese culture, as applied and operating in organizations—in this case, a bank.

Pygmalion in the Classroom, by Robert Rosenthal and Lenore Jacobson. New York: Holt, 1968. 240 pages.

Some of the material in this book is treated in Chapter 3, but there is a great deal more of considerable interest in the study. Recommended both for supervisors and educators.

The Dragons of Eden, Speculations on the Evolution of Human Intelligence, by Carl Sagan. New York: Ballantine, 1977. 271 pages.

Important for its discussion of the human brain and of computers. If time is pressing, read at least Chapter 2 (pages 21–49). Sagan is accorded high praise by dozens of writers.

The World Challenge, by Jean-Jacques Servan-Schreiber. New York: Simon & Schuster, 1980. 302 pages.

A superb book in total, but the manager and supervisor will do well to study part III (pages 133–240), which has to do with the United States vis-à-vis Japan.

Japan as Number One: Lessons for America, by Ezra F. Vogel. Cambridge, Mass.: Harvard University Press, 1979. 272 pages.

Among the best of the many books about Japan in relation to the United States. Some of the comparisons of the two countries are shocking (to an American), but all are meticulously buttressed with factual material. Vogel does not suggest that Americans become like the Japanese but rather that we learn from Japan as we once learned from Europe. A must for any supervisor or manager.

Magazines and Journals

Listing journals of probable value to supervisors is not too easy. All that follow will usually contain at least one article of interest in each issue, and most of them will have several. There are, of course, many other useful periodicals that may occasionally have a good article, or that may have several in one issue. Sometimes such occasional articles or numbers may be quite valuable. But to list every periodical that might possibly have good supervisory material at one time or another would make our starter set much too long. The ones listed here should prove useful, at least as a beginning.

Harvard Business Review. Published bimonthly by the Graduate School of Business Administration, Harvard University. About ten to twelve articles; lots of advertising; 180 pages. The magazine is aimed generally at business and industrial concerns; however, definitive articles on new developments in the management field usually appear in this publication. Not necessarily easy reading—as advertised by the magazine itself. Considered by many the "best" of management magazines.

Management Review. Published monthly by the American Management Association, Inc. "The Month's Best in Business Reading." Contains digests from various magazines and newspapers; usually two to three special features plus a dozen digests; short summaries of other timely articles; a book review section. About 80 pages, digest size.

Training and Development Journal. Official magazine of the American Society for Training and Development. (Formerly the *Training Directors Journal.*) Monthly, about seventy to eighty pages, ten to fifteen articles, twelve to fifteen training research abstracts, classified ads, book reviews.

Personnel Journal. "The Magazine of Industrial Relations and Personnel Management." Published by the Personnel

Journal, Inc., Swarthmore, Pa. Monthly (July-August issues combined). About 60 pages, eight to ten articles, book reviews, help and positions wanted advertisements, and special features.

Personnel. Published bimonthly by the American Management Association. About 80 pages, eight to ten articles, book reviews, special features.

Personnel Administration. Journal of the Society for Personnel Administration. Contains six to eight original articles, book reviews, and several special features. Bimonthly. About 60 pages.

Supervisory Management. Published monthly by the American Management Association, Inc. Contains about twelve to fourteen features and digests of articles from other magazines in about equal numbers; book review section, cases, notices of laws, etc. About 60 pages. Somewhat less sophisticated than *Management Review.*

Supervision. "The Magazine of Industrial Relations and Operating Management." Published by Supervision Publ. Co., Mt. Morris, Ill. Appears monthly. Of value primarily to industrial shop foremen. About 30-35 pages.

Nation's Business. Published monthly by the U.S. Chamber of Commerce. Usually contains one to three specific management articles.

Bits & Pieces. Published monthly (always 24 pages) by the Economics Press, Inc. "A monthly mixture of horse sense and common sense about working with people," says the cover page. A mix of excellent statements about supervision, plus anecdotes and jokes that are delightful.

17

Change

It has been said that human beings are inherently creative—
that this is one of the fundamental attributes that separates
us from the animals. A desire to create or to innovate is what
we count on to bring about changes in our society, changes
that will make things better for us—and for our children.

It seems that there are two major matters, among others,
operating to block the expression of our creative genius, if I
may call it that. Both of them are equally human. Let us
consider these:

The first is *the kinds of organizations we build.* Every organization we set up, every policy we declare, every procedure we
require to be followed, every rule we promulgate, every
method we specify, every regulation, every way of operating—is set up to make things go in a certain way, and *in that
way only.* By one means or another, in our organizations, we
require our people to conform, to conduct their work and
themselves in accordance with the set rules and regulations
and policies, to follow the prescribed methods and procedures, and to play a specified and well-bounded part within
the organization structure. Those who follow faithfully the
organizational lines get selected for promotion. Those who
do not get selected out.

The very factors that act to help us achieve success in organization—in educational, governmental, industrial, business, and other organizations—are the same factors that act
to block any change.

People on the outside can frequently see what is happening more easily than those on the inside, who, if we had a good organization to start with, are prone to defend it. Eventually the time comes when outside forces making for change become unbearable. Our organization creaks and groans. People in it, at various levels and locations, begin to make accommodating changes surreptitiously. They begin, as we say, to *bootleg* changes, hoping of course they they will not be caught in the act. They are, in fact, desperately trying to keep an organization running that they can now see is in a rut—which has been defined by one humorist as a grave with the ends knocked out. What a commentary on human endeavor, that useful and valuable organizational changes must often be bootlegged.

Ultimately, of course, as our organization begins to come apart, we have a reorganization, sometimes known as a *shake-up*. Usually this is performed by a new person at the helm. The new person is the new broom, as we say, that sweeps clean. There is commonly a task force, privy to the new broom, that meets under heavy security wraps, in a back room, to develop a new organization. In proportion to the tightness of the security, rumors run wild. The grapevine hums and throbs as people gather in small, nervous groups to speculate about the impending changes. "Have you heard?" they say to each other. "I hear Jones is out . . . Smith is leaving . . . Henderson is in . . . Anderson is to be the next head . . . I have it from a guy who knows a guy . . . Where does *this* leave us? Where does this leave *me?*" The work of the organization slows down, comes to a grinding halt.

At last our task force report is out. Our worst fears may—or may not—be realized. The old formerly successful structure is swept away; new policies are set forth and new procedures replace old ones. And the overriding rule of the new organization, created if you like out of chaos, is *no change*. If the new organization is to succeed, there must be no deviation from the new rules, the new policies, the new procedures, the new structure. The only commandment left over from the old organization is a curiously familiar one: hereafter, *do things in this way and this way only.* This being the law, we are in for the same old cycle all over again. In a very real sense, most of our reorganizations simply signal the onset of a disease we might call organizational paralysis complicated by operating ossification.

The second major matter operating to block change has to do with the very human characteristic of forming habits.

We—all of us—develop habits. Some of these we recognize, some we do not. The ones we are fully aware of, we may change as we see the need. But the habits we have *that we do not know we have* may go on controlling our behavior without change. These are only simple habits: But *note:* The human propensity for forming habits, personal habits—many of them unknown and unrealized by us—is extended to the way we do our jobs, the way we operate in our positions, and the way in which we manage our organizations. Human habits become customs. And both habit and custom operate against change. This is the way we do it because this is the way we've always done it; and this is the only way to do it because we have always done it this way. How very similar this sounds to the overriding commandment of organizations; namely, do things *this* way and *this way only.*

Thus, both by the nature of the organizations we build and by the habits and customs we develop, we, ourselves, prevent change from taking place. In the short run, our organizations may succeed—a clear-cut indication that our rule of conformity, of no-deviation, no change, is working. In the long run, as our world changes but our rules of conformity do not, our organizations must inevitably fail.

Now, how can we break out of these prisons we build for ourselves? How can we provide for necessary changes in our organizations, in our policies, in the way we do things?

Certainly, there is no easy answer for such questions, and, with Harvey Sherman, we must say, "It all depends":

1. *If* we have an organization of the authoritarian type, we

can see that we need to get new leaders, or get the leaders we have to develop better habits. An authoritative organization is one in which the few people in the managing group at the top call the shots, set the policies, police the procedures, and generally preserve the status quo. All the rest of the people in the organization either conform or get out. Here, as one of my former associates used to say, you must have a few first-class funerals before you're likely to get much change. The alternative is for the managing heads to change their behavior. This alternative, I sometimes think, is far less likely to take place, although I am bound to say that it *does* occur, even if rarely.

2. If, on the other hand, we have a highly participative type of organization, including *real* freedom of speech, a well-oiled *communication system,* and an attitude on the part of all the people in it that *they* want the organization to succeed as strongly as does the managing group of leaders, then conditions are right for change whenever the need becomes clear. In such an organization—and there are some in the United States—if a stream of information and new knowledge reaches *all* the people, all of it indicating a need for the organization to change direction, or operations, or its structure, the people are likely to be not only willing to consider proposals for change but also willing to recommend changes themselves.

The seedbed for needed change, in other words, is a *condition* that needs to exist *throughout* an organization. The managing heads of at least some of the businesses, industries, governmental agencies, and educational and religious organizations in this country have constructed and operated just such organizations with success. I say that if this *has* been done with a few, it can be done anywhere. The newest, the best scientific knowledge we have from the fields of psychology, sociology, anthropology, and human behavior all points in this direction. Let us, then, all of us, prepare for change— the one constant force in this world in which we live.

Index